THE
Everyday
GOURMET

FAST & FABULOUS
MICROWAVE
RECIPES

Enjoy the magic of microwave!

JANE TRITTIPO

To Tom,
my husband
whose love,
support,
encouragement,
unending patience
and belief in me
helped
my dream become
a reality

ACKNOWLEDGMENT

Though self-published, this book was by no means all my own creation. I want to thank my supportive friends in AAUW, P.E.O., Lyra Chapter of Easter Seals and St. Timothy's Episcopal Church. To Maggie Crum, Food Editor, Contra Costa Times; Jo Harberson, my proofreader; Steve Schwein, my computer expert; Jill Brennan, Alberta Herfurth, Georgia Whitaker, and to my many, many students, thanks for your encouragement.

I want to give special thanks to my family. Without the encouragement of our two daughters, Karen and Lynn, this book would still be just a dream. Without my husband Tom and his patient ways as well as recipe testing abilities, I never could have published The Everyday Gourmet. This book would really look like helpful-hands-at-home without the graphic design expertise of our daughter Karen and her husband David. I am especially grateful to my parents and grandparents, who, though no longer living, influenced my cooking interests, and always encouraged me to pursue my dreams.

CONTENTS

A MOST IMPORTANT MESSAGE TO A MOST IMPORTANT PERSON—-YOU!!

This is not **MY** microwave cookbook, it is **YOUR** microwave cookbook. It will help you understand **YOUR** microwave and solve some problems you may have been experiencing. During my five years teaching microwave-food processor classes in my home, I have learned:

1   Most people don't read instructions.

2   Most people aren't ready or willing to take the time to learn how and why the microwave works, and how it can work for them.

3   Most people buy a microwave oven, bring it home, warm up a cup of coffee and say "this is great!" They throw away the box and the book that came with the marvelous coffee warmer and soon wonder why this huge-tin-box-with-a-window came into their lives. They begin to feel guilty about never using it except of course to reheat coffee, and so they start to search for help.

BECAUSE people don't like to read instructions, I have purposely made the recipes in this book as concise and complete as possible. I have written only one recipe per page and provided space for you to write comments. Remember this is **YOUR** book, not mine. I begin each recipe with a note of encouragement and if appropriate, a little background regarding the recipe. If you should cover a dish the book tells you to do so. If you should cook it uncovered the book says nothing.

Learning to use the microwave is very much like using a computer. Until you train the operator, (that's **YOU**) this machine that can do wonderful things will just take up space on your overcrowded counter. I have tried to include a wide variety of recipes that the microwave can handle beautifully, so that you may finally taste success and start to think about adapting favorite family recipes.

This is the most important bit of advice in the whole book and could help you avoid disasters and help you become an avid microwave cook. It Is:

DETERMINE THE WATTAGE OF YOUR MICROWAVE

How do you do that? First look in the book that came with your microwave. If you don't have the book, look on the metal plate near the cord on the back of your microwave. If your microwave is built in don't despair, for I have a little kitchen chemistry lesson that will help you determine the wattage of your microwave.

1   Pour 4 3/4 cups or 1 liter of water into a large micro-safe bowl.

2   Take temperature of water and adjust so that it is between 60 and 70 degrees F.

3   Microcook the water on High Power 1 minute 3 seconds.

4   Take the temperature of the water.

5   Subtract the beginning temperature from the ending temperature and multiply by 38.8.
(Example: (end temp) 86 - (beg temp) 69 = 17 x 38.8 = 657.6. The wattage of this microwave is 650 watts)

Now that you know this most important information, write the wattage of your microwave in the space below.

Most microwave recipes, and those in this cookbook, give timings for a 700 watt microwave. If yours has a lower wattage look at the chart directly below where you entered your wattage. It tells you the additional minutes or seconds you will need to cook.

THE WATTAGE OF MY MICROWAVE OVEN IS:_____

600-700 WATTS	500-600 WATTS	400-500 WATTS
15 sec.	18 sec.	20 seconds
30 sec.	35 sec.	45 sec.
1 min.	1 min. 15 sec.	1 min. 30 sec.
2 min.	2 min. 30 sec.	2 min. 50 sec.
3 min.	3 min. 30 sec.	4 min. 15 sec.
4 min.	4 min. 50 sec.	5 min. 45 sec.
5 min.	6 min.	7 minutes
6 min.	7 min. 15 sec.	8 min. 30 sec.
8 min.	9 min. 30 sec.	11 min. 15 sec.
10 min.	12 min.	14 minutes

Locate the book that came with your microwave or order one from the manufacturer of your microwave oven. Read it, as it contains valuable information for you. Try to find a chart or information regarding power level, wattage and percent. You need this information to avoid disasters.

Fill in the chart on the next page with the information you find. When a recipe says to cook on Medium Power (50%) make certain your Medium Power is 50%. Mine isn't! My Medium Power is 70% and I overcooked three caramel flans before I discovered my problem.

POWER	WATTS	PERCENTAGE
HIGH	_____	_____
MED HIGH	_____	_____
MEDIUM	_____	_____
MED LOW	_____	_____
LOW	_____	_____
WARM	_____	_____
DEFROST	_____	_____

Here's how the microwave oven works: When you turn on your microwave to cook food, microwaves 5-6 inches long and as big around as your finger are dispersed from the magnetron tube. These ripply waves pass through the microsafe containers and through the food. As they pass through the food, they vibrate the molecules billions of times a second. This vibration is the energy that cooks the food in the microwave. That's the reason we cook by time and volume of food rather than by temperature. There is no temperature in the microwave, only the temperature of food that is being cooked.

To get **YOU** started with **YOUR** new cookbook. I suggest you read through Chapter 1 - 101 QUICK TRICKS. I have included hints on cooking and unusual uses for the micro-wave. You'll find tricks about shoe polish, dog food, ironing and nail polish in the microwave.

After Chapter 1, find a recipe you like and try it. Don't try to cook a whole meal in the microwave until you get more accustomed to using it. If you are afraid to try real cook-ing, not just reheating, try the Tabbouleh Salad recipe (see page # in index) All you do is add boiling water to several wonderful ingredients and you end up with a delicious middle eastern salad.

I am most enthusiastic about the many wonderful things a microwave can cook to perfection. I hope that I have inspired you to learn to cook in your microwave. **YOU** have a most wonderful cooking machine and time saver sitting right there in your kitchen. Do take the time to learn to use it. It is my intent that **YOU** will find the ideas, recipes and menus in this book helpful and that **YOU** will soon become a proficient microwave cook.

Jane Trittipo

1

101 QUICK TRICKS

1 **ACORN SQUASH - CUTTING** To cut acorn squash more easily, microcook on High Power 1-2 minutes uncovered. Let stand 2 minutes before cutting open.

2 **ALMONDS - BLANCHING** Place 3/4 cups almonds and 1 cup water in a microsafe bowl. Microcook on High Power 3 minutes. Drain. When cool, rub almonds to remove skins.

3 **APPLE PIE WITH CHEESE - WARMING** Place 1 apple pie wedge on a microsafe serving plate, top with cheddar cheese slice and microcook on High Power 15-20 seconds.

4 **AVOCADOS** Soften by microcooking on Medium Power (50%) 2 minutes; turn over and microcook on Medium Power (50%) 1 minute.

5 **BABY FOOD** Remove metal jar lid and microcook on High Power 10-15 seconds or until warm. Be sure to test before feeding baby..

6 **BACON COOKING** Place bacon slices on bacon cooking rack or microsafe plate and cover with paper towel to prevent splatters. Microcook on High Power 1 minute per slice of bacon.

7 **BACON SLICES - SEPARATING** Separate slices more easily by microcooking the entire package on High Power 30-45 seconds

8 **BAGELS** Split bagel and top with a small piece of cream cheese. Microcook on Medium Power (50%) 30 seconds, spread cheese over bagel and enjoy.

9 **BARBECUED CHICKEN** Partially precook chicken by microcooking on Medium Power (50%) 3 minutes per pound. Put on grill and reduce grilling time by 1/3.

10 **BARBECUED HAMBURGERS** Grill extra hamburgers or other meats and freeze. For just-grilled flavor, micro-cook one frozen hamburger patty on Medium Power (50%) 3-4 minutes.

11 **BEANS** To hasten preparation and omit overnight soaking: place 2 cups dried beans and 2 cups water in a microsafe casserole. Cover tightly with plastic wrap and microcook on High Power 15 minutes. Let stand 15 minutes. Remove plastic wrap and add 2 cups hot water. Recover and let stand 1 hour. Drain and use in any recipe calling for soaked beans.

12 **BRANDY** Warm brandy for flaming by pouring 1/4 cup into a microsafe bowl. Microcook on High Power 10-15 seconds. Pour into a large silver or glass ladle and ignite. Pour flaming over cake or fruit. Warmed brandy can also be poured directly on dessert and ignited immediately.

13 **BREAD OR ROLL** To warm 1 piece of bread or 1 roll, place on a paper towel or cloth napkin to absorb moisture. Microcook on High Power 8-12 seconds, no longer. If you overcook you'll create rubber.

14 **BREAD CRUMBS** Toast bread crumbs by placing 1 cup crumbs on a microsafe plate and microcooking on High Power in 1 minute intervals, stirring after each minute. Microcook to desired toastiness.

15 **BREAD - FROZEN** Thaw frozen bread by placing 2 slices on paper or cloth towel and microcooking on Medium Power (50%) 1 minute.

16 **BROWN SUGAR** Soften rock-hard brown sugar by placing box in microwave and microcooking on High Power 30-45 seconds.

17 **BUTTER - CLARIFYING** Place 1/4 pound butter in a 2 cup microsafe measure. Cover loosely with paper

towel and microcook on High Power 2 minutes. Skim solids from surface of liquid and discard. Pour off clear liquid carefully, leaving the milky solids behind.

18   **CABBAGE** Loosen leaves for cabbage rolls by coring and wrapping head in plastic wrap and microcooking on High Power 2-3 minutes.

19   **CEREAL** Measure 1/3 cup quick rolled oats, 2/3 cup water and 1/8 teaspoon salt into a large serving bowl. Microcook on High Power 1 1/2 minutes, cover and let stand 3 minutes.

20   **CHOCOLATE** Place 1-ounce square wrapped chocolate, seam side up in the microwave. Microcook on Medium Power (50%) 2 1/2 to 3 1/2 minutes. It will not look melted until stirred. Unwrap and transfer to bowl with a rubber spatula. You can melt chocolate this easy way and never dirty a dish.

21   **CHOCOLATE CHIPS - MELTING** Place 6 ounces chocolate chips in a microsafe bowl, microcook on High Power 2 minutes, stir and continue to cook on High Power in 30 second intervals. Don't be surprised if they continue to look like chips; chocolate retains its shape though melted. Be sure to stir well.

22   **CHOCOLATE CURLS** Place unwrapped block of chocolate in microwave and microcook 7-10 seconds. Scrape off curls with a vegetable peeler, holding chocolate block over dessert to be decorated,.

23   **CHOCOLATE LEAVES** These easy-to-make chocolate leaves add a very special touch to cakes and pies. Microcook 1 square of semi-sweet chocolate on High Power 1 minute or until melted. With pastry or artist's brush, brush chocolate on underside of stiff green leaves (camellia or rose leaves are perfect). Place chocolate coated leaves on tray in refrigerator or freezer. When hardened, carefully peel leaf from chocolate, being careful not to melt chocolate from warmth of your hands. A pattern of the veins of the leaves will be imprinted in the chocolate.

24 **CITRUS JUICE** Lemons and oranges are easier to squeeze and yield more juice if pierced with a knife and microcooked on High Power 45-60 seconds.

25 **CLAY COOKERS** If you have a clay cooker, by all means use it in your microwave. Soak before cooking stews, veal roasts etc. If using conventional recipe, reduce liquid slightly and decrease cooking time by 2/3.

26 **COCONUT - TOASTING** Place 1/3 cup coconut in a microsafe bowl and microcook on High Power 1 1/2 minutes.

27 **CORN ON THE COB** Husk 2 ears corn, spread with butter and sprinkle with salt and pepper. Wrap each ear in plastic wrap and microcook on High Power 3-4 minutes. Let stand 3 minutes and serve wrapped.

28 **CREAM CHEESE** To soften, place a 3-ounce block of cream cheese in a microsafe dish. Microcook on Medium Power (50%) 30-60 seconds or until soft. An 8-ounce block will soften if cooked on Medium Power (50%) 1-1/2 minutes.

29 **EGGS** Hard cook eggs for chopping and adding to salads or casseroles. Crack egg into lighly greased custard cup, prick yolk with toothpick, cover with plastic wrap and microcook on Medium Power (50%) 1 1/2-2 minutes or until white is set and yolk is almost set; let stand, covered, 1 minute.

30 **FINGER TOWELS** An easy way to impress guests. Wet 4-8 wash cloths with water that is scented with co-

logne or lemon juice. Wring out, fold or roll and place in a wicker basket. Microcook on High Power, 2-3 minutes.

31 **FINGERNAIL POLISH** Loosen stuck non-metal cap by microcooking on High Power 5-10 seconds.

32 **FINGER PAINTS** Blend 1 cup water into 1/2 cup cornstarch in large microsafe bowl. Add 2 more cups water and microcook on High Power 8-9 minutes or until thickened, stirring every 2 minutes. Pour 1/2 cup thickened mixture into each of six small bowls and stir in 3 drops desired food coloring per bowl.

33 **FLOWERS - DRYING** Drying flower petals in the micro-wave is quickly done and there is good color reten-tion. Lavender heads: spread in a single layer on a paper towel. Place in the microwave with 1/2 cup water in a microsafe bowl. Microcook on High in one minute intervals until dry. Let stand 10 minutes. For rose petals: spread in a single layer on a paper towel. Place in microwave with 1/2 cup water in a microsafe bowl and microcook on High Power 1 minute or in 10 second intervals until dry. Use in making potpourri.

34 **FOODS - KEEPING AT SERVING TEMPERATURE** Place casserole or serving dish in microwave and micro-cook on lowest power setting (10%) 30-60 minutes or more.

35 **FRUITS - DRY** Soften dried fruits and plump prunes by placing 2 tablespoons water and 1 cup fruit in a microsafe bowl, cover with plastic wrap and micro-cook on High Power 1 minute, or until plump and soft. Stir, let stand 2-3 minutes and drain.

36 **FRUITS - FRESH, PEELING** Microcook peaches, plums or nectarines on High Power 15-30 seconds to loosen skin and make fruit easier to peel.

37 **GELATIN** For crystal clear gelatin, combine flavored gelatin and 2 cups water in a microsafe bowl. Microcook on High Power 2 1/2 - 3 minutes or until boiling. Stir to be certain gelatin is dissolved.

38 **GELATIN - ADDING FRUITS, VEGETABLES OR NUTS** If gelatin has set too firmly to add fruits, vegetables or nuts, microcook on Medium Power (50%) 1 - 1 1/2 minutes or until soft enough to add desired ingredients. Refrigerate until firm.

39 **GROUND MEAT - COOKING** Crumble meat into a microsafe plastic colander placed in a larger microsafe bowl. Microcook on High Power 4-5 minutes, per pound of meat. Stir once during cooking and cook just until meat is no longer pink. This method prevents hard lumps from forming by draining out excess fat as soon as it is liquified. Microwaves are attracted to fat, sugar and water, thus lumps form if you cook ground beef without draining the grease.

40 **GROUND MEAT - FREEZING** Form fresh ground beef into a ball before wrapping and freezing. When you defrost the ball in the microwave, you will have a uniform mass that will defrost more evenly rather than a rectangular mass with thin edges which will actually start to cook before the center is thawed.

41 **GROUND MEAT - MEAT LOAF** Using favorite meat loaf recipe, shape loaf into a ring leaving center open. It will cook more evenly and more quickly than the traditional loaf form. Leave space around edges for juices to drain, cover loosely with waxed paper and microcook on High Power 5 minutes per pound. Remove juices with a turkey baster and serve.

42 **HERBAL VINEGARS** Place herb sprig (tarragon, basil, etc.) or skewered garlic cloves into decorative sterilized bottles. Microcook red or white wine vinegar on High Power just until boiling. Using funnel, pour vinegar into bottle, cover tightly and let stand at least 10 days before using or giving as gifts. Use approximately 1 tablespoon of herbs for each cup of vinegar.

43 **HERBS - DRYING** Place fresh herbs (parsley, basil, thyme, tarragon etc.) on a microsafe plate with paper towels over and under the herbs. Microcook on High Power 2-3 minutes per half cup herbs, stopping cooking as soon as they feel dry and crumbly. Exact timing depends on the herb and its freshness. Store in tightly covered jar.

44 **HONEY - CRYSTALLIZED** Liquify crystallized honey by placing in a microsafe container and microcooking on High Power 1 1/2 minutes per cup of honey, stirring every 30 seconds.

45 **HONEY - LIQUIFYING** Before trying to measure honey for use in a recipe, remove lid, place container in microwave and microcook one minute. It will pour like water.

46 **HONEY - PLASTIC CONTAINERS** Containers were not made for microwaving. You can however, microcook to soften honey for one minute but no longer. Don't do as a friend did and microcook for 4 minutes. Her container disappeared into a plastic-honey puddle.

47 **HOT COMPRESS** For sore muscle relief, dampen a towel with cold water, wring out sightly and microcook on High Power 1 minute or until very warm to the touch.

48 **HOT DOGS - COOKING** Place hot dog weiner on a microsafe plate and microcook on High Power 45 seconds. Place in bun, wrap with napkin or paper towel and microcook on High Power 10-15 seconds. This eliminates overcooked rubberized bun and cold hot dog.

49   **HOT DOGS - THAWING 1/2 PACKAGE** Mold aluminum foil smoothly around portion of frozen package not to be used and microcook on Medium Power (50%) 1 1/2-2 1/2 minutes, or until unshielded side is soft and cool to touch but not icy. Remove defrosted portion and return frozen remainder to freezer.

50   **ICE CREAM** Soften hard ice cream by microcooking in its container on Medium Power (50%) 30 seconds per quart.

51   **ICE CREAM TOPPINGS** Remove lid from ice cream topping jar and microcook on High Power 45-60 seconds. Stir and ladle over ice cream.

52   **IRONING** To dampen items quickly and evenly, sprinkle water lightly on tablecloths, napkins etc. Place in a 1 gallon plastic garbage bag and twist open end to close loosely. DO NOT use metal twist tie. Microcook on High Power 1 minute or until warm to the touch.

53   **JUICES - FROZEN** Thaw frozen concentrated fruit juices by removing metal lid from one end, placing container in microwave and microcooking on High Power I minute. Pour partially thawed concentrate into serving container and add water. Stir briefly to dissolve.

54   **LEMON PEEL OR ZEST - DRIED** Sprinkle lemon or orange peel on a microsafe plate and microcook on High Power 1-2 minutes. Store in an airtight container and use in recipes calling for zest or in making potpourri.

55   **MEAT MARINATING** To speed marinating of meat, place marinade in a microsafe bowl and microcook on High Power 1-2 minutes per cup of marinade. Add meat to the warm marinade and let stand for at least 30 minutes.

56   **MILK - SCALDING** Pour 1 cup milk in a microsafe container. Microcook on High Power 2 -2 1/2 minutes.

57   **MOLASSES** Before trying to measure molasses, place open jar in microwave and microcook on High Power 45-60 seconds. It will pour like water.

58   **MULTIPLE DISHES - COOKING** To cook several different foods at the same time (i.e. a casserole, a vegetable and bowl of soup), add together the recommended cooking times for all the items, subtract 25% from the total and use this as the approximate total cooking time. Check each item at end of cooking period and cook longer if necessary.

59   **MUSHROOMS - DEHYDRATE** Place 1/2 pound sliced mushrooms in a single layer on a paper towel. Micro-cook on High Power, 6-8 minutes, rearranging slices halfway through cooking time. Mushrooms are dehydrated when semi-leathery to touch and no moisture appears when sliced. Store in an airtight container. Rehydrate by combining with liquid in recipe or soaking in tepid water 5-15 minutes to plump.

60   **NUTS - BROWNING** Because of their high fat content and the fact that microwaves are attracted to fats, nuts brown quickly in the microwave. Place 1/2 cup nuts (almonds, walnuts, pecans, pine nuts etc.) on a microsafe plate. Microcook on High Power 3-4 minutes. Stir while cooking as they can burn in spots.

61   **NUTS - SHELLING** This simple technique makes shelling nuts easy. Place unshelled nuts in a microsafe bowl with 1 cup water. Cover with plastic wrap and microcook on High Power 3-4 minutes, or until water boils. Let stand 1 minute, drain and spread out to cool. Crack open carefully as shells will contain hot water.

62 **ODORS** To remove lingering fish or cooking odors from the microwave, simply measure 2 tablespoons lemon juice or 2 tablespoons baking soda in 1 cup water. Microcook on High Power 5 minutes. Wipe walls clean.

63 **ONIONS - ALMOST TEAR-FREE CHOPPING** Cut off both root and stem end of onion. Place the unpeeled onion in the microwave and microcook for 1 minute. Don't overcook, as onion will become mushy. Let cool slightly before peeling and chop as usual, but with a minimum of tears.

64 **OYSTERS - SHUCKING** Soak oysters in cold water 3 hours. Place 6 oysters in a microsafe casserole, cover with plastic wrap and microcook on High Power 45 seconds or until shells have opened. Continue to cook unopened ones, checking every 15 seconds. Insert knife near hinge to open completely, then cut away muscle from the shell. Use oysters in your favorite recipe. This method of shucking is not recommended if you wish to eat them raw.

65 **PANCAKES** Reheat frozen leftover pancakes by placing on paper towels and microcooking on Medium Power (50%) 45 seconds per pancake.

66 **PARAFFIN - DO NOT TRY TO MELT IN MICROWAVE** Paraffin has no water, sugar or fat and therefore won't melt in the microwave.

67 **PASTA - REHEATING** Reheat pasta by microcooking on High Power 1-2 minutes per cup pasta.

68 **PEACHES - EASY PEELING** Place 2-3 peaches in a microsafe bowl, add 3 Tablespoons water, cover with plastic wrap and microcook on High Power, 1-2 minutes.

69 **PET FOOD** Take the chill off pet food by placing in a microsafe bowl and microcooking on High Power 15-30 seconds..

70 **POPCORN - FRESHEN** A bowl of soggy or stale pop-corn can be freshened by microcooking on High Power 30-45 seconds. Let stand l-2 minutes to crisp.

71 **POPCORN - POPPING** Use only approved micro-safe popcorn popper or commercially prepared microwave popcorn packages. Do not use paper bag to pop corn, as it may catch fire because of intense heat buildup.

72 **POTATO CHIPS - FRESHEN** Place stale potato chips in a microsafe bowl or basket. Microcook on High Power 30-45 seconds. Let stand 1-2 minutes to crisp.

73 **POTATOES - BAKED** Microcook 4 medium potatoes on High Power 10 minutes, wrap in foil, let stand at least 5 minutes. Will hold heat up to 45 minutes.

74 **POTATOES - CRISP BAKED** Microcook 4 medium potatoes on High Power 10 minutes. Bake in a 350 degree conventional oven 10 minutes or until as crisp as you like.

75 **POULTRY** Place chicken or turkey parts on a micro-safe plate with meatier portions on outside edge. Cover with plastic wrap and microcook on High Power. Timing: 1 boneless chicken breast-3 min-utes; 3 boneless chicken breasts-6 minutes; 3 chicken breasts with bone in-9 minutes. Chicken or turkey parts generally cook in 6-7 minutes per pound, turning over parts once during cooking. Poultry is done when juices run clear after piercing with a fork.

76 PRETZELS - FRESHEN Place stale pretzels in a micro-safe bowl or basket. Microcook on High Power 30-45 seconds. Let stand 1-2 minutes to crisp.

77 RAISINS Plump or soften raisins by placing 1 cup raisins in a microsafe bowl. Sprinkle over raisins 1 tablespoon water. Cover with plastic wrap. Microcook on High Power 1 1/2 minutes, stir and let stand a few minutes.

78 RECIPE CONVERSION - HALVING OR DOUBLING Halve a microwave recipe by using half the amount of all ingredients and microcooking 2/3 the original time. Double a microwave recipe by doubling the dry ingredients, adding 1 3/4 the amount of liquid and microcooking the doubled recipe 1 1/2 to 1 2/3 the original time.

79 RICE Place 1 cup long grain rice with 2 cups water in a large microsafe serving bowl. Cover tightly with plastic wrap and microcook on High Power 15-17 minutes. Fluff with fork, re-cover with plastic wrap and let stand until serving time. Cooking rice in the microwave eliminates need for stirring, avoids the danger of the rice boiling dry and makes fluffier rice. Cooking it in a serving dish is most convenient. Refer to index for Perfect Rice Recipe.

80 ROLLS - REHEATING Place 6-8 dinner rolls in a wicker or straw basket lined with a linen or cotton napkin. Microcook on Defrost 45 seconds. The linen or cotton witll absorb the steam and keep the rolls crisp.

81 SAUCES Never need constant stirring and cook faster in the microwave because energy enters from all sides. Measure, mix and microcook in the same container for easy cleanup. Refer to index for chapter on sauces.

82   **SAUSAGE LINKS** Take 4 sausage links and pierce skin to prevent popping due to steam buildup. Place on a microsafe plate and microcook on High Power 2 1/2 - 3 minutes.

83   **SESAME SEEDS** Spread 1/2 cup sesame seeds on a microsafe plate. Microcook on High Power 2-3 minutes, stirring once. Butter may be added to seeds, but you must stir more often to prevent burning.

84   **SHOE POLISH - LIQUID** Reconstitute dried liquid polish by adding 2-3 tablespoons water to bottle and microcooking on High Power 5-10 seconds. Shake bottle to blend. Repeat, if necessary, until liquid reaches desired consistency.

85   **SHOE POLISH - PASTE** Soften dried, crumbly polish by microcooking in a non-metal container on High Power 5-10 seconds.

86   **SHRIMP - COOKING** Place 1 pound unshelled fresh or frozen shrimp in a microsafe dish. Add 1/2 cup water, 1/4 teaspoon salt, 1 bay leaf and 2 lemon slices. Cover with plastic wrap. Microcook on High Power 5-6 minutes, stirring once. Drain and rinse in cold water to stop cooking. For peeled shrimp follow same procedure, microcooking on High Power 4-5 minutes.

87   **SILICA GEL** Reactivate silica gel after it has become pink, indicating loss of absorbency, by microcooking on High Power until blue color returns. Use the same silica gel for several years by microcooking whenever gel turns pink.

88   **SOAP BALLS** Make instant soap balls by softening remains of soap bars in a little water and microcooking on High Power 1-2 minutes. When slightly cooled and soft, mold into a ball or balls.

89 **SOUP** Reheat refrigerated soup in soup bowls covered with plastic wrap by microcooking on High Power until heated through. I cup reheats on High Power in 2 1/2-3 1/2 minutes. 2 cups reheat on High Power in 6-7 minutes.

90 **SYRUP** Heat syrup for pancakes or waffles by pouring syrup into a microsafe pitcher and microcooking on High Power 45-60 seconds.

91 **TACO SHELLS** Heat taco shells by microcooking 10-12 precooked crisp taco shells on High Power 1-3 minutes, or until warm.

92 **TEMPERATURE PROBE OR INSTANT READ MICROWAVE THERMOMETER** These are wonderful aids in microcooking and reheating without guess work. If you have a built-in temperature probe learn to use it for foolproof microcooking. Read your manual for full instructions. Your microwave will actually cook or reheat to your pre-determined temperatures and shut off. Instant read microwave thermometers are purchased separately. Use the instant read thermometer to check whether food has reached desired temperature. Use following time and temperatures for reheating, placing probe in center:

Sandwich	Med. High (70%)	110°
Casserole (stir once)	Med. High (70%)	150°
Soup	High Power	160°
Pie (probe horizontal)	High Power	110°
Syrup/Sundae topping	High Power	130°
Gravy	Med. High (70%)	140°
Sauces and Dips	Med. High (70%)	140°
Vegetables	Med. High (70%)	150°

93 TOMATOES - PEELING Core 1 large, ripe tomato and place in microwave. Microcook on High Power 10-20 seconds, let stand 5 minutes to cool. Peel will come off easily.

94 TORTILLAS Wrap 6-8 flour tortillas in a dampened paper towel and microcook on High Power 1 minute to warm and soften. Repeat process if they cool.

95 UNFLAVORED GELATIN - DISSOLVING Sprinkle 1 envelope gelatin in 1/4 cup cold water in a micro-safe bowl. After softened, microcook on High Power 30-45 seconds. Proceed with recipe.

96 VEGETABLES - FROZEN Cook frozen vegetables in original package. Boxed vegetables: Stand box on edge, not on largest side, so microwaves can more easily penetrate vegetables. Microcook on High Power 5 minutes, let stand 3 minutes. Open box, drain, season and spoon vegetables into serving bowl or on individual plates. If further heating is needed, return to microwave and cook on High Power in 1 minute intervals. Plastic Pouch Vegetables: Slash pouch to allow steam to escape. Microcook on High Power 5 minutes, let stand 3 minutes. Drain, season and serve, or reheat as necessary in 1 minute intervals.

97 WAFFLES Place two room temperature waffles between paper towels on a microsafe plate and microcook on High Power 25 seconds.

98 WARM DINNER PLATES OR SERVING DISHES Lay 1 sheet of paper towel over microsafe plate or serving dish, sprinkle with a few drops of water, microcook on High Power 1 minute.

99 WOODEN SPOONS When preparing any recipe that requires microcooking and stirring, stir with a wooden spoon, leaving the spoon in the container while cooking. It's convenient for stirring and keeps your counter clean.

100 YEAST To avoid killing the yeast because water temperature is too hot, place water called for in recipe into a microsafe bowl with probe or instant read microwave thermometer. Microcook on High Power to 115 degrees. Remove water, add yeast and proceed with recipe.

101 YEAST DOUGH - RAISING Raise yeast dough in a quarter of the time. Pour 3 cups water into a microsafe bowl, microcook on High Power 5-6 minutes or until boiling. Place bowl of boiling water in corner of microwave oven. Place dough in medium glass bowl loosely covered with waxed paper in microwave next to the bowl of water. Select lowest power setting, Warm or 10%, and microcook for 20 minutes Remove dough from oven and let stand covered with waxed paper 20 minutes. Shape dough as recipe directs, repeating raising procedure if required.

2

APPETIZERS

Warm Brie with Pine Nuts
Prosciutto Wrapped Asparagus with Dill Mayonnaise
Teriyaki Shish Kabob Appetizers
Artichoke Dip
Bacon and Pineapple Spears
Mini Reubens
Beef Roll-Ups
Chicken Bolognese Style
Brandied Chicken Liver Paté
Perpetual Cheese Spread
Bacon and Walnut Appetizer Pie
Roasted Garlic
Hot Crab Dip
Cheesy Clam Dip
Shrimp Mousse
South of the Border Dip
Super Simple Nachos
Mexican Fondue
Rosemary Walnuts

Guaranteed to impress! The pine nuts add a special flavor and crunch.

WARM BRIE WITH PINE NUTS

1 one-pound round Brie Cheese
3 tablespoons butter or margarine
1/3 cup pine nuts
butter crackers

1   Place butter and pine nuts on a microsafe plate. Microcook on High Power one minute. Cook and stir in 30 second intervals until nuts are light brown: 3-4 minutes.

2   Cut Brie round in half horizontally. Place each half skin side down on a separate microsafe serving plate. Sprinkle toasted pine nuts over both rounds and cook on Medium Power (50%) 3-5 minutes, or until soft enough to dip into with crackers.

3   Serve immediately with butter crackers.

4   Any kind of nuts can be substituted for the pine nuts, or nuts and butter could be omitted altogether.

Serves 8-10

This is an elegant appetizer for special guests.

PROSCIUTTO WRAPPED ASPARAGUS WITH DILL MAYONNAISE

1 pound fresh, thin asparagus
1/4 pound prosciutto

1   Break off ends of asparagus and wash. Arrange asparagus in a large, round microsafe dish with tips in center.

2   Cover with plastic wrap and microcook on High Power for 3 1/2 to 4 1/2 minutes, just until tender but still a bit crisp.

3   Let cool and wrap with prosciutto slices, barberpole fashion.

4   Arrange on a tray in a fan, and place a small bowl of dill mayonnaise at base of the fan for dipping.

Makes 18-24 pieces

<u>Dill Mayonnaise</u>:

2 egg yolks
2 teaspoons dried dill weed
1 tablespoon lemon juice
1/4 teaspoon salt
1 tablespoon white wine vinegar
1/8 teaspoon white pepper
1 teaspoon Dijon mustard
1 1/4 cups vegetable oil

PROSCIUTTO WRAPPED ASPARAGUS
WITH DILL MAYONNAISE   *continued*

1   In processor bowl fitted with steel blade combine the
     egg yolks, lemon juice, wine vinegar, mustard, dill
     weed, salt and pepper. Pulse briefly.

2   With processor running, very slowly pour oil through
     feed tube. If your processor pusher has a hole in it,
     pour the oil into the pusher while processor is on and
     the oil will be added automatically in a thin stream.

3   If you do not have a processor, whisk egg yolks,
     lemon juice, vinegar, mustard, dill weed, salt and
     pepper in a mixing bowl. Continue to whisk while
     adding oil drop by drop.

4   Other herbs, nuts etc. may be substituted for the dill
     weed if you prefer.

Makes approximately one cup. (Will keep several weeks if
refrigerated.)

This is a colorful, tasty appetizer. Try it for a holiday gathering.

TERIYAKI SHISH KABOB APPETIZERS

1 pound sirloin steak (trim off fat)
1 20-ounce can pineapple chunks
1 small green pepper, cut in small squares
cherry tomatoes (1 per skewer)
disposable wooden skewers

Marinade:

1/4 cup soy sauce
2 tablespoons sherry
3 tablespoons brown sugar
1 clove garlic, minced
1 small chunk fresh ginger, minced
2 teaspoons flour

1   Cut steak into bite-size pieces, about the same size as the pineapple chunks.

2   Combine soy sauce, sherry, brown sugar, garlic, ginger and flour. Add beef cubes and pour into a plastic bag and close tightly. Marinate at room temperature for a least one hour, rotating the bag occasionally.

3   Thread individual skewers with a cube of beef, a green pepper chunk, a pineapple cube and a cherry tomato. Arrange half the kabobs (20) in a circle, on a microsafe plate in a spoke fashion, with meat chunks on outer edges of the plate.

4   Microcook 20 kabobs on High Power 4-5 minutes. Repeat cooking procedure with remaining kabobs.

Makes approximately 40 kabobs. (These colorful appetizers look especially nice fanned out on a pretty tray.)

A fancy serving dish enhances the presentation of this easy appetizer.

ARTICHOKE DIP

1 6-ounce jar marinated artichoke hearts, undrained
1 4-ounce can diced green chiles
1 cup mayonnaise
1/2 cup grated Parmesan cheese
Butter crackers or cubes of French bread

1   Coarsely chop artichoke hearts and combine with diced green chiles, mayonnaise and Parmesan cheese in a microsafe serving dish.

2   Microcook on High Power 2-4 minutes or until bubbly. Serve warm with butter crackers or cubes of crusty French bread for dipping.

Serves: 6-8

A simple flavorful combination of meat and fruit.

BACON AND PINEAPPLE SPEARS

12 slices bacon
12 slices pineapple spears, fresh or canned
toothpicks

1   Wrap each bacon slice around a pineapple spear
     and fasten with a toothpick. Place on microsafe
     bacon cooking rack or paper towel- lined microsafe
     plate and microcook on High Power for 6 minutes.

2   Turn spears over and microcook 5-6 more minutes or
     until bacon is crisp.

Makes 12 pieces

Hide these or hungry guests will eat them before they're cooked. They are best when microcooked just enough to melt the cheese.

MINI REUBENS

36 slices party-size rye bread
1/2 cup Thousand Island dressing
1/4 pound thinly sliced corned beef
1 8-ounce can sauerkraut, drained
36 small slices Swiss cheese (2″ x 2″)
36 dill pickle slices

1   Spread bread with Thousand Island dressing and top with corned beef that has been coarsely chopped. Spoon sauerkraut over the corned beef. Place a slice of Swiss cheese over the sauerkraut and top with a dill pickle slice.

2   Arrange 12 mini sandwiches at a time in a circle on a large microsafe plate. Microcook on Medium Power (50%) 2 1/2 to 3 minutes, or until cheese is melted. (To cook 6: Microcook on Medium Power (50%) 1 1/2 to 2 minutes.)

Makes: 36 mini sandwiches

These will disappear quickly at your next party.

BEEF ROLL-UPS

1 tablespoon chopped onion
1 clove garlic, minced
1 teaspoon Worcestershire sauce
1/4 cup soy sauce
1 tablespoon sugar
1/4 teaspoon ground ginger
1/4 teaspoon salt
1/2 pound top round or sirloin steak cut diagonally in thin
    strips
1 6-ounce can whole water chestnuts
Toothpicks or wooden skewers

1   Combine onion, garlic, Worcestershire sauce, soy
     sauce, sugar, ginger and salt in a mixing bowl.

2   Add meat strips and marinate 30 minutes or more,
     stirring occasionally.

3   Halve water chestnuts.

4   Drain meat strips on paper towel. Wrap 1 meat strip
     around a water chestnut half and secure with a
     toothpick or wooden skewer.

5   On a microsafe plate, arrange 10 roll-ups in a circle.
     Microcook on High Power 3-4 minutes, rotating dish
     1/4 turn, halfway through cooking. Serve hot. Re-
     peat with remaining roll-ups.

Makes approximately 20 pieces

For a smashing presentation, fan these out on a serving piece or a basket tray.

CHICKEN BOLOGNESE STYLE

5 chicken breast halves, skinned, boned and flattened
5 tablespoons butter or margarine
2 tablespoons chopped Italian parsley
2 cloves garlic, minced
1/4 pound pancetta (Italian bacon) diced and micro-
    cooked on High Power 3-4 minutes
3 tablespoons pine nuts
2 sun-dried tomatoes, diced and softened in olive oil
3 tablespoons olive oil
2 tablespoons freshly ground black pepper

1   Combine butter, parsley, garlic, pancetta, pine nuts and sun-dried tomatoes, just until mixed.

2   Lay chicken breasts on counter overlapping them. Spread the butter-nut-pancetta mixture over the breasts.

3   Roll chicken jellyroll style into a log and tie at 1 inch intervals with string. Roll in olive oil and then black pepper.

4   Wrap the chicken log in plastic wrap and microcook on High Power 11-12 minutes, or until chicken is no longer pink. Let stand 5 minutes.

5   Cut in small diagonal slices. Serve 3 slices on individual plates as a first course or skewer slices on bamboo skewers and arrange decoratively on a large tray or basket.

Serves 6-8

Impress your friends with this lovely paté! They will think you've spent hours and you've only spent minutes!

BRANDIED CHICKEN LIVER PATE´

1 pound chicken livers, cleaned
1/4 cup water
1/4 medium onion, chopped
2 large sprigs parsley, chopped
2 tablespoons brandy
8 tablespoons butter or margarine
1/2 teaspoon salt
1/4 teaspoon ground allspice
1/8 teaspoon ground mace
Pumpernickel bread triangles
Cornichons (or other miniature pickles)

1   Place livers and water in a microsafe bowl, cover with plastic wrap and microcook on High Power until livers lose pink color, 8-10 minutes. (You will hear some popping but that is OK). Drain livers.

2   Combine livers, onion, parsley, brandy, 2 tablespoons butter, salt, allspice and mace into processor bowl fitted with the steel knife. Process until smooth or purée in blender.

3   Add 6 tablespoons butter, 1 tablespoon at a time, while machine is running. Spoon liver mixture into a pâte´ crock or suitable serving dish and refrigerate until serving time.

4   Serve with triangles of pumpernickel bread and cornichons.

Makes approximately 2 cups. (Keeps several days in the refrigerator or can be frozen).

This is a great recipe for using bits and pieces of cheese.

PERPETUAL CHEESE SPREAD

4 ounces cheese, grated (Swiss, cheddar, jack, mozzarella,
     etc. or any combination of)
1 3-ounce package cream cheese
1/2 cup nuts, chopped (almonds, walnuts, pecans,
     cashews, etc)
2 tablespoons butter or margarine
1/2 teaspoon dried basil
Salt
2 tablespoons brandy, cognac or sherry
Crackers, toast triangles, vegetable slices, etc.

1   Place cream cheese in a microsafe bowl and micro-cook on High Power, uncovered for 1 minute.

2   Add other cheeses, nuts, butter, basil, salt and brandy.

3   Refrigerate spread in a tightly covered container. As the spread is used, add any cheeses, nuts or herbs. If the flavor becomes too sharp, add cream cheese or butter. To add to the spread, place in a microsafe bowl and microcook on Medium Power (50%), uncovered, just until softened. Add new ingredients and mix well.

4   The spread may be served cold on crackers, toast triangles or vegetable slices. Or serve them warm by microcooking on High Power until bubbly.

Makes approximately 1 cup (This spread will keep for several months in the refrigerator. Add brandy, cognac or sherry every 6-8 weeks.)

This is a dip-like pie with an interesting combination of flavors.

BACON AND WALNUT APPETIZER PIE

5 slices bacon
1 8-ounce package cream cheese
2 tablespoons milk
2 tablespoons instant minced onion
2 tablespoons chopped green pepper
1/2 cup sour cream
1/8 teaspoon pepper
1/4 cup coarsely chopped walnuts
Assorted crackers

1   Place bacon slices on microsafe bacon cooker, cover with paper towel to avoid spattering, and microcook on High Power until crisp, 5-6 minutes. Crumble and reserve.

2   Place cream cheese and milk in a large microsafe bowl. Microcook on High Power 1-2 minutes to soften.

3   Add onion, green pepper, sour cream and pepper to the cream cheese and mix well. Spread evenly on an 8 inch pie plate or microsafe decorative serving plate. Cover loosely with waxed paper and micro-cook on High Power 3-4 minutes.

4   Sprinkle with walnuts and reserved crumbled bacon. Serve with assorted crackers.

Serves 8-10

A popular California appetizer quickly prepared in your microwave.

ROASTED GARLIC

4 heads garlic
1/3 cup chicken broth
3 tablespoons olive oil
thin slices of French bread
Butter or Boursin type cheese

1   Place the garlic heads, chicken broth and olive oil in a large microsafe bowl. Cover with plastic wrap and microcook on High Power for 6-8 minutes, cooking longer if bulbs are large.

2   Remove from microwave and let stand, covered, for 10 minutes.

3   Cut tips off entire head of garlic. Garlic cloves may be eaten by scraping the pulp out with your teeth or can be squeezed on French bread spread with butter or a Boursin type cheese.

4   Roasted garlic may also be served as an accompaniment to roasted meats or chicken.

Serves 4

Another appetizer that you cook and serve in the same bowl!

HOT CRAB DIP

3 8-ounce packages cream cheese
2 6-ounce cans crab meat or 3/4 pound cooked
    crabmeat
1 clove garlic, minced
1/2 cup mayonnaise
2 teaspoons prepared mustard
1 cup dry white wine
2 teaspoons powdered sugar
1 tablespoon chopped onion
1 teaspoon seasoned salt
Party rye slices or chips for dipping

1   Place the 3 blocks of cream cheese in a microsafe serving bowl and microcook on High Power 2-3 minutes, until softened.

2   Add crab, garlic, mayonnaise, mustard, wine, powdered sugar, onion and salt. Mix well, and microcook on High Power 2 minutes, stir, and continue to cook on High Power until bubbly, stirring every 30 seconds.

Serves 10-12

A little different from the usual 'clam dip'

CHEESY CLAM DIP

2 tablespoons minced onion
2 tablespoons butter or margarine
1 7-ounce can minced clams, undrained
1 tablespoon catsup
Dash of Tabasco
1 cup diced American process cheese
2 tablespoons chopped black olives
1 teaspoon Worcestershire sauce
1 16-ounce bag round corn chips for dipping

1   Place onions and butter in microsafe bowl. Cook
     on High Power 1 minute or until tender.

2   Add clams, catsup, Tabasco, cheese, olives and
     Worcestershire sauce. Microcook on Medium
     Power (50%) 3 minutes. Stir and continue to cook
     on Medium Power stirring and cooking in 1 minute
     intervals, until smooth and hot. Pour into decora-
     tive bowl and serve with round corn chips for
     dipping.

Serves 8-10

This gelatin-based mousse is a snap to make in your microwave.

SHRIMP MOUSSE

1 envelope gelatin
1/4 cup cold water
1 8-ounce package cream cheese
1 10 3/4 - ounce can cream of mushroom soup
1 cup mayonnaise
1 7-ounce can shrimp bits and pieces
1/2 cup chopped celery
1/4 cup chopped onion
Butter crackers

1   Soften the gelatin in the cold water.

2   Place the cream cheese and soup in a microsafe bowl and microcook on High Power 2-3 minutes or until very warm. Remove from microwave and stir until smooth.

3   Add softened gelatin to soup-cheese mixture and microcook on High Power 1 minute. Add mayonnaise, shrimp, celery and onion. Mix well and pour into a water rinsed mold, cover and refrigerate.

4   Unmold by rimming the edge with a knife and immersing mold briefly in hot water. Place serving plate on top and quickly invert. Serve with butter crackers as an appetizer or pour into individual molds and serve with crackers on individual plates as a first course.

Serves: 12-14

Your guests will really love this rather hearty appetizer.

SOUTH OF THE BORDER DIP

1 8-ounce package cream cheese
1 medium onion, chopped
1 4-ounce can chopped green chiles
1 14-ounce can Mexican chili without beans
1 2 1/4-ounce can sliced ripe olives, drained
8-ounces Monterey jack cheese, grated
1 16-ounce bag taco chips for dipping

1   Place the cube of cream cheese in a microsafe pie plate or quiche dish. Microcook on High Power 1 minute or until soft enough to spread evenly over bottom of dish.

2   Spread the chopped onions over the cream cheese, then sprinkle the chiles over the onions. Spoon the Mexican Chili over this layer and sprinkle ripe olives and grated Monterey Jack cheese on top. Micro-cook on High Power 3-4 minutes or until bubbly.

3   Serve warm with taco chips for dipping.

Serves: 6-8

Can't get much simpler than this!

SUPER SIMPLE NACHOS

1 16-ounce package corn chips for dipping
1 18-ounce can refried beans
1 7-ounce jar taco sauce, hot or mild
1 4-ounce can chopped ripe olives
1 cup cheddar cheese, grated

1   Scoop up a little of the refried beans onto each corn chip. Place 18 chips on a large microsafe plate, arranging chips in a circle.

2   Pour sauce sparingly over chips. Sprinkle olives and grated cheese over chips. Microcook on High Power 2-3 minutes or until bubbly. Repeat cooking process with rest of the chips.

3   These can also be cooked on a paper plate and transferred to a serving tray.

Makes approximately 72 nachos

This is a great chili con queso recipe, extremely fast and easy, and you cook it in the serving bowl!

MEXICAN FONDUE

2 pounds process American cheese
1 7-ounce can green chili salsa
1 4-ounce can chopped green chile peppers
1 large tomato, chopped
1 16-ounce bag tortilla chips for dipping

1   Place cheese in a microsafe serving bowl and micro-cook on Medium Power (50%) for 4-5 minutes, stir and continue to cook on Medium Power (50%) at 3 minute intervals, until cheese is melted and smooth when stirred.

2   Add green chili salsa, chile peppers and chopped tomato to the melted cheese and microcook, on Medium Power (50%) for 3-4 minutes or until heated through.

3   Place serving bowl on a tray and surround with tortilla chips, reheating in microwave on Medium Power when necessary. For individual servings, spoon fondue into small ramekins and place on dinner plate with chips for dipping alongside. Use as an accompaniment to a Mexican type entrée with refried beans etc.

Serves 10-12

These tasty nuts disappear quickly. Toss a few in a green salad for added pizazz.

ROASTED ROSEMARY WALNUTS

1/4 cup unsalted butter
1 tablespoon dried rosemary, crumbled
1/4 teaspoon salt
1/8 teaspoon cayenne pepper
2 cups walnut halves (8 ounces)

1   Combine butter, rosemary, salt and cayenne in a microsafe shallow casserole. Microcook on High Power 1 minute.

2   Add walnuts and toss to coat. Microcook on High Power, 5-8 minutes, stirring often, until lightly browned and aromatic.

Makes 2 cups

3

SOUPS

Hearty Italian Sausage Soup
Chilled Cucumber Soup with Walnuts
Vichyssoise
Tomato Sip
Marvelous Mushroom Soup
Corn Chowder
Carrot-Tarragon Soup
Broccoli Bisque
Walnut Soup
Creamy Clam Chowder
Easy Easy Crab Bisque
Greek Lemon Soup (Avgolemono)
Chili Con Queso Soup
Chicken Stock

A main course soup for family or friends. Just add a green salad and crusty french bread and dinner's ready.

HEARTY ITALIAN SAUSAGE SOUP

1 1/2 pounds mild Italian sausage
2 cloves garlic, minced
2 large onions, chopped
1 28-ounce can Italian style tomatoes
3 14-ounce cans beef broth
1 1/2 cups dry red wine
1/2 teaspoon dried basil
3 tablespoons chopped parsley
1 medium green pepper, chopped
2 medium zucchini, sliced 1/4 inch thick
3 cups uncooked bow tie noodles (5 ounces)
Grated Parmesan cheese

1 Cut sausage into 1/2 inch lengths. Brown on cooktop or in browning dish in microwave oven.

2 Place sausage and any drippings in a 3-4 quart microsafe casserole, along with onion and garlic. Microcook on High Power for 2-3 minutes, or until vegetables are slightly softened.

3 Add wine, tomatoes and juice, beef broth and dried basil. Microcook on Medium Power (50%) 15 minutes. Cool in refrigerator.

4 Skim off the fat layer that forms. Add parsley, pepper, zucchini and noodles. Microcook on High Power, covered, 12-15 minutes or until noodles are tender. Serve with grated Parmesan cheese.

Serves 4-6

The chopped walnuts in this chilled soup add a nice crunch and a subtle flavor.

CHILLED CUCUMBER SOUP WITH WALNUTS

4 cucumbers, peeled, seeded and sliced
3 cups chicken stock
1 tablespoon chopped onion
1/2 teaspoon dried dill weed
1/2 teaspoon salt
Dash white pepper
2 cups sour cream or plain yogurt
1/2 cup chopped walnuts
Thin slices of unpeeled cucumber or fresh dill sprigs for
        garnish

1   Place the cucumbers, chicken stock and onion in a
     large microsafe bowl or casserole. Microcook,
     covered, on High Power 8-9 minutes or until boiling.
     Microcook on Medium Power (50%) 3-5 minutes, until
     cucumbers are tender. Cool.

2   Purée cucumber mixture in a food processor or
     blender. Add dill weed, salt and pepper. Stir in sour
     cream and walnuts.

3   Chill and adjust seasonings. Serve cold, garnished
     with paper-thin slices of unpeeled cucumber or fresh
     dill sprigs.

Serves 6-8

Another old favorite easily prepared in the microwave.

VICHYSSOISE

6 green onions, sliced (white and green part)
4 tablespoons butter or margarine
8 medium white potatoes, peeled and thinly sliced
1 tablespoon salt
5 cups chicken broth
2 cups half-and-half
Generous grating of fresh nutmeg
White pepper to taste
1 cup whipping cream
Fresh chives for garnish

1   Place onions and butter in a large microsafe casse-
      role. Microcook on High Power 3-4 minutes until
      onions are limp.

2   Add potatoes and chicken broth and microcook
      covered on High Power 10 minutes. If the potatoes
      are not tender after 10 minutes, cook them longer,
      one minute at a time, testing and stirring after each
      minute, until tender.

3   Purée potato mixture in food processor or blender.
      Add half-and half, nutmeg and pepper. Chill well.

4   Before serving check seasoning and adjust. Stir in
      whipping cream and serve in bowls garnished with
      sprigs of fresh chives or sprinkle with chopped chives.

Serves 6

No spoons necessary for this soup! Nice to serve to a big crowd, as guests can wander around talking and sipping.

TOMATO SIP

2 10-ounce cans beef bouillon
2 1/2 cups tomato juice
1 tablespoon lemon juice
6 whole cloves
1/4 teaspoon dried basil
1 bay leaf
1/2 teaspoon Worcestershire sauce
Lemon slices for garnish or
Celery sticks for stirrers

1   Combine the bouillon, tomato juice, lemon juice, cloves, basil, bay leaf and Worcestershire sauce in a large microsafe casserole or bowl.

2   Microcook on High Power, 8-10 minutes or until mixture begins to boil.

3   Remove bay leaf and cloves; serve in mugs or bowls. Garnish with lemon slices or serve with celery stalks as stirrers.

Serves 6 (Multiple batches can be made to serve a large crowd. However, be certain not to boil as the lemon flavor intensifies and becomes bitter.)

If you like mushrooms, you'll love this creamy smooth creation.

MARVELOUS MUSHROOM SOUP

1 pound fresh mushrooms, thinly sliced
6 cups chicken broth
2 egg yolks
1/2 cup sour cream
1 tablespoon sherry
Salt and pepper

1   Combine mushrooms and chicken broth in a large microsafe bowl. Microcook covered, on High Power 15 minutes or until mushrooms are tender.

2   Process in small batches in processor or blender until smooth. Return mushroom broth mixture to the microsafe bowl.

3   Mix egg yolks, sour cream, sherry, salt and pepper. Add to the mushroom broth mixture and microcook covered, on Medium Power (50%) 6 minutes or until hot. (170 degrees on an instant read thermometer).

Serves 6

Another oh-so-easy but oh-so-good soup!

CORN CHOWDER

3 slices raw bacon, diced
1/4 cup finely chopped onion
1 16-ounce can cream style corn
1/4 cup water
1 cup milk
1/2 teaspoon salt
1/4 teaspoon pepper
Chopped parsley for garnish

1   Combine onion and diced bacon in microsafe bowl, cover and microcook on High Power 2-3 minutes, stirring several times. Drain off grease.

2   Add corn, water, milk, salt and pepper to the cooked onion and bacon. Microcook uncovered on High Power 4-5 minutes, or until serving temperature is reached.

3   Allow to stand covered 2-3 minutes before serving. Garnish with chopped parsley.

Serves 2-3

This carrot-tarragon combination is wonderful! Present it with a sprig of fresh tarragon on top.

CARROT-TARRAGON SOUP

4 cloves garlic, minced
1 medium yellow onion, chopped
10 tablespoons butter or margarine
10 cups chicken stock
2 tablespoons dried tarragon
1/4 tablespoon white pepper
6 large carrots, peeled and grated
Sprigs of fresh tarragon for garnish

1   Place garlic, onion and 8 tablespoons butter in a 4 quart microsafe casserole. Microcook on High Power 4-6 minutes or until vegetables are soft.

2   Add 2 cups of the chicken stock, dried tarragon and white pepper. Microcook on High Power 8-10 minutes until volume is reduced by one-half.

3   Add remaining chicken stock and grated carrots. Microcook on Medium Power (50%) 15-20 minutes, or until carrrots are well cooked.

4   Pour soup into processor fitted with steel blade (or a blender). Process in batches until smooth. Return soup to microsafe 4 quart casserole.

5   Add remaining 2 tablespoons butter, stir and microcook on Medium Power (50%) 5-8 minutes or until hot.

6   Serve in individual bowls and garnish with sprigs of fresh tarragon.

Serves 6-8

Your microwave really performs on this one. Microcook the broccoli and the white sauce easily and quickly. Try it!

BROCCOLI BISQUE

4 10-ounce packages frozen chopped broccoli
1/2 cup chopped onion
4 cups chicken broth
4 tablespoons butter or margarine
2 tablespoons flour
4 teaspoons salt or to taste
Dash pepper
1 tablespoon lemon juice
4 cups half-and-half
Pretzel sticks

1   Combine broccoli, onion and chicken broth in a 4 quart microsafe casserole. Microcook on High Power 10-12 minutes or until boiling. Cover and microcook on Medium Power (50%) 5 minutes.

2   In another microsafe bowl, combine flour and butter. Microcook on High Power 45 seconds. Stir in half-and half.

3   Purée the broccoli mixture in small batches in a processor or blender.

4   Combine the broccoli mixture with white sauce, salt, pepper and lemon juice. Reheat in microwave on High Power until serving temperature is reached. (170 degrees on an instant read thermometer). Adjust seasonings and serve in mugs with pretzel sticks as stirrers.

Serves 4-5

An unusual soup to serve special guests. The walnut flavor is enhanced by the hot seasonings.

WALNUT SOUP

6 cups beef stock or bouillon
2 tablespoons butter or margarine
2 tablespoons flour
1 1/2 cups finely ground walnuts
1/2 teaspoon Worcestershire sauce
2 dashes Tabasco
2 tablespoons Madeira
Freshly ground black pepper
Salt

1   Pour beef stock into a large microsafe bowl and microcook on High Power until boiling, 8-10 minutes.

2   Place butter in another microsafe bowl and micro-cook on High Power for 30 seconds. Stir flour into butter until a smooth sauce is produced.

3   Add bouillon, ground walnuts, Worcestershire sauce and Tabasco to the flour-butter mixture and micro-cook on Medium Power (50%) 15 minutes.

4   Add Madeira to the soup and microcook on Medium Power (50%) 5 minutes or until serving temperature is reached (170 degrees on an instant read thermometer). Add salt to taste.

Serves 6

You'll love the flavor of this chowder and you'll be amazed at how quickly it is prepared using your microwave.

CREAMY CLAM CHOWDER

4 slices bacon, cut in 1 inch squares
1 medium yellow onion, chopped
1 pound (3 medium) raw potatoes, peeled and chopped
1 clove garlic, minced
1/2 teaspoon salt
1/4 teaspoon white pepper
1 teaspoon Worcestershire sauce
4 drops Tabasco
2 7-ounce cans minced clams, undrained
2 cups half-and-half

1   Place bacon squares in a microsafe casserole and microcook on High Power 4-5 minutes or until crisp. Do not drain grease.

2   Add chopped onion, chopped potatoes, garlic and juice from clams to bacon in the casserole. Cover with plastic wrap and microcook on High Power 10 minutes, stirring after 5 minutes.

3   Add salt, white pepper, Worcestershire sauce, Tabasco and half and half to the potato mixture. Cover with plastic wrap and microcook on High Power 4-5 minutes or until serving temperature is reached. (170 degrees on an instant read thermometer).

4   Stir in clams and serve immediately.

5   To reheat, microcook on Medium Power (50%) 4-6 minutes, depending on the volume to be reheated. Do not boil as this will toughen the clams.

Serves 4-6

Yes, this is "a can of" recipe, but you can fool even the gourmet cooks with this microfast recipe.

EASY EASY CRAB BISQUE

1 10-ounce can pea soup
1 10-ounce can tomato soup
1 cup cream
1/2 pound crab or 1 6-ounce can crabmeat, rinsed,
     drained and flaked
3 tablespoons sherry

1   Combine pea soup, tomato soup and cream in a
     large covered microsafe casserole or bowl. Micro-
     cook covered on High Power 8-10 minutes, or until
     boiling. Stir occasionally during cooking.

2   When hot, add crab and sherry, cover and micro-
     cook on Medium Power (50%) 3-4 minutes to heat
     through.

Serves 4

This is a lovely first course soup. The lemon zest adds a welcome touch of tartness.

GREEK LEMON SOUP (Avgolemono)

2 14-ounce cans chicken broth
2 tablespoons uncooked long grain rice
1 teaspoon grated lemon zest
2 tablespoons lemon juice
1 egg, beaten
4 thin slices lemon
snipped parsley

1   Combine broth and rice in a large microsafe casserole. Cover with plastic wrap and microcook on High Power 14-16 minutes. Let stand 15 minutes.

2   Combine lemon zest with egg and lemon juice. Pour a small amount of the hot broth into the egg mixture, stirring constantly. Pour egg mixture into the remaining hot broth.

3   Microcook the soup mixture on Medium Power (50%) 5-6 minutes, being careful not to boil.

4   Serve in individual soup bowls topped with a thin slice of lemon and a sprinkle of snipped parsley.

Serves 4

Another South of the Border favorite.

CHILI CON QUESO SOUP

2 tablespoons butter or margarine
1 large onion, chopped
1 28-ounce can peeled tomatoes, with liquid
1 4-ounce can diced green chiles
1 2-ounce jar diced pimentos
1/2 pound Monterey jack cheese, grated
1/2 pound cheddar cheese, grated
Salt and pepper to taste
Cilantro or parsley for garnish

1   Combine butter and onion in a microsafe bowl, microcook on High Power 7 minutes, stirring occasionally.

2   Cut tomatoes into pieces. Add tomatoes with their liquid, chiles and pimentos to the onion and butter, blend well. Cover with plastic wrap and microcook on High Power until soup comes to a full boil; 9-10 minutes.

3   Stir in cheeses and continue to cook uncovered on High Power until cheeses are melted, 1-2 minutes.

4   Add salt and pepper to taste. Serve hot with a sprinkle of cilantro or parsley.

5   To reheat soup, microcook on Medium Power (50%) 8-10 minutes, or until serving temperature. This lower power will prevent overcooking the cheeses.

Serves 4-6

There is nothing like homemade chicken stock. Let your microwave help you make it quickly.

CHICKEN STOCK

2 pounds chicken bones, wing tips, etc.
1 quart water
1/2 cup chopped celery
1/2 cup chopped onion

1   Chop bones into 1-2" pieces.

2   Place bones, water, celery and onion in a 3 quart microsafe bowl. Cover with plastic wrap and micro-cook on High Power 30-40 minutes.

3   Cool slightly and strain. Refrigerate or freeze. Use as a base for soups, sauces, etc.

Makes 2 cups

4

SALADS

Tabbouleh
White Bean and Ham Salad
Beef Salad Olé
Oriental Chicken Salad
Molded Spring Salad
Mustard Mold
Potato Salad Niçoise
Lettuce Wedges with Warm Blue Cheese Dressing
Wilted Greens Salad
Calamari Salad
Raisin, Pecan and Wild Rice Salad
Garlic Croutons

The wonderful flavors of this favorite bulgur wheat salad belie the ease of preparation in your microwave. Just boil water and add all these wonderful ingredients.

TABBOULEH

1/2 cup olive oil
6 tablespoons lemon juice
1/4 cup chopped fresh mint leaves
1/4 cup chopped fresh parsley
3 green onions, chopped (including green portion)
1 clove garlic, minced
3/4 teaspoon ground cumin
3/4 teaspoon salt
1/4 teaspoon freshly ground black pepper
1 cup medium bulgur wheat
1/2 cup water
1/2 cup pine nuts
2 medium ripe tomatoes, seeded and finely chopped
Romaine lettuce
Fresh mint leaves for garnish.

1   Whisk together the olive oil, lemon juice, mint leaves, parsley, green onion, garlic, cumin, salt and pepper. Set aside.

2   Pour water into a large microsafe bowl and micro-cook on High Power 2-3 minutes or until boiling. Add bulgur and stir to moisten evenly. Immediately stir in previously made dressing, pine nuts and tomatoes. Set aside for at least 8 hours, or refrigerate overnight to allow bulgur to soften and absorb dressing.

3   To serve, line a serving bowl with romaine lettuce leaves and fill with tabbouleh. Garnish with mint leaves.

Serves 8-10 (Tabbouleh will keep well for several days if covered and refrigerated.)

Instead of the usual overnight soaking of beans, let your microwave help you prepare this flavorful salad in 3 hours. Read on!!

WHITE BEAN AND HAM SALAD

2 cups dried white beans
1 medium-size purple onion, halved, peeled and sliced thin
1 cup chopped Italian parsley
1 pound cooked ham trimmed and cut into 1 inch cubes
Salt
Freshly ground pepper

Dressing:

1 egg
1/3 cup Dijon mustard
2/3 cup red wine vinegar
salt and freshly ground black pepper, to taste
6 garlic cloves, minced
2 cups olive oil

1   Place beans in a microsafe bowl, add 2 cups water and cover tightly with plastic wrap. Microcook on High Power 15 minutes. Remove from microwave and let stand covered for 5 minutes. Uncover and add 2 cups very hot water. Re-cover and let stand for 1 hour. Drain.

WHITE BEAN AND HAM SALAD   *continued*

2 Place drained beans in a microsafe casserole, add 4 cups water, cover with 2 sheets of plastic wrap and microcook 40 minutes. Let stand covered 30 minutes.

3 While beans are 'standing' combine dressing ingredients. Drain beans and immediately toss with 1 cup dressing.

4 Add onion, parsley, ham cubes and season to taste with salt and pepper. Toss again, cover and refrigerate.

5 To serve, allow salad to return to room temperature. Toss again, correct seasoning and add more dressing if you like.

Serves 6-8

A wonderful dinner salad for a hot summer evening.

BEEF SALAD OLÉ

1 1/2 pounds boneless top sirloin
1/2 cup picante sauce
2 teaspoons cornstarch
1 tablespoon vegetable oil
3/4 teaspoon ground cumin
1/2 teaspoon garlic salt
1/4 teaspoon pepper
2-3 ripe avocados
2-3 oranges, peeled, sliced and chilled
Lettuce
1/2 cup pitted whole ripe olives
Fresh cilantro leaves

Dressing:

1/2 cup picante sauce
1/2 cup sour cream
1/2 cup chopped tomato
2 tablespoons chopped green
Onions
1 tablespoon chopped cilantro
Hot pepper sauce, optional

BEEF SALAD OLÉ
continued

1   Combine dressing ingredients and refrigerate.

2   Partially freeze sirloin. Slice into 1/8 inch strips.

3   Combine picante sauce and cornstarch. Place the mixture in a plastic bag and add beef strips. Close bag securely. Marinate beef for 20-30 minutes, turning bag occasionally to blend mixture thoroughly.

4   Place oil and ground cumin in a microsafe baking dish. Add beef with marinade, stirring to coat. Cover loosely with waxed paper and microcook on Medium Power (50%) 9-11 minutes or until beef is only slightly pink. Stir in garlic salt and pepper.

5   Slice avocado and brush with lime juice. Arrange on lettuce-lined individual serving plates along with sliced oranges. Arrange beef mixture in center of plate and ladle over the dressing. Garnish with olives and cilantro leaves.

Serves 6

A fast and fabulous luncheon salad for special guests!

ORIENTAL CHICKEN SALAD

4 chicken breasts (bone in)
8 tablespoons sesame oil
3 tablespoons soy sauce
2 teaspoons sugar
1 teaspooon grated ginger root
1 teaspoon dry mustard
1 garlic clove, minced
1 teaspoon salt
1/2 package rice sticks
1/8 teaspoon white pepper
Vegetable oil for deep frying
4 tablespoons rice vinegar
1/2 cup sliced almonds
1 head iceberg lettuce, shredded
2 tablespoons sesame seeds
3/4 cup fresh coriander leaves
4 green onions, chopped

1   Place the chicken breasts, bone side down on the
      edge of a microsafe plate, cover with plastic wrap
      and microcook on High Power 7 minutes. Uncover,
      turn breasts over, re-cover and cook on High Power 2
      minutes or until juices run clear, not pink. Let stand
      until cool enough to remove meat from bones.

ORIENTAL CHICKEN SALAD   *continued*

2   Combine soy sauce, ginger and garlic. Shred
         chicken and marinate in the soy mixture a few hours
         or overnight.

3   Place almonds and sesame seeds on a microsafe
         plate. Microcook on High Power in 2 minute intervals
         until brown.

4   Fry rice sticks in hot oil on range top, being certain the
         oil is very hot. Remove rice sticks before they brown.
         (This will take only a few seconds.)

5   Prepare salad dressing by combining sesame oil,
         sugar, mustard, salt, pepper and rice vinegar.

6   Combine the marinated chicken with the shredded
         lettuce, chopped onions and coriander. Toss well.
         Drizzle dressing over salad ingredients, lightly mix in
         the rice noodles, toasted almonds and sesame seeds.
         Serve immediately.

Serves 8

Even jello salads are easier to make with a little help from your microwave.

MOLDED SPRING SALAD

1 3-ounce package lemon-flavored gelatin
1 cup hot water
3/4 cup Sauterne or other dry white wine
3 tablespoons white wine vinegar
2 tablespoons sugar
Pinch salt
1 10-ounce package frozen mixed vegetables
1/2 cup finely diced celery
2 tablespoons chopped green onion
2 tablespoons chopped parsley

1   Pierce bag or box of frozen mixed vegetables. Place in microwave standing on edge. Microcook on High Power 5 minutes. Microcook just until crisp tender, drain and reserve.

2   Dissolve gelatin in hot water; add wine, wine vinegar, sugar and salt. Microcook on High Power 1 minute to be sure gelatin and sugar are dissolved. Chill.

3   When slightly thickened add previously cooked vegetables, celery, onion and parsley. Pour into decorative mold which has been rinsed in cold water. Chill until firm. (Individual molds can also be used.)

4   To serve, unmold on bed of crisp salad greens and offer mayonnaise flavored with prepared horseradish as an accompaniment.

Serves 6

This creamy mustard mold is nice to serve with ham or a cold sliced meat platter.

MOLDED MUSTARD CREAM

1 envelope gelatin
1/3 cup water
3/4 cup sugar
3 tablespoons dry mustard
1/4 teaspoon salt
2/3 cup vinegar
4 eggs, beaten
1 cup whipping cream, whipped

1   Soften gelatin in water.

2   Combine sugar, mustard and salt in a medium size microsafe bowl. Add vinegar and beaten eggs.

3   Add gelatin to sugar-egg mixture and microcook on High Power 4-6 minutes, stirring every 2 minutes. Cook until thickened and of custard consistency. Cool.

4   When cooled, fold in whipped cream and pour into decorative mold, individual molds or a ring mold. Store in refrigerator until ready to serve.

Serves 10-12

A fancy potato salad for your next picnic.

POTATO SALAD NIÇOISE

Dressing:

1/2 cup extra-virgin olive oil
1/4 cup fresh lemon juice
2 tablespoons red wine vinegar
3 anchovies rinsed and patted dry
3 tablespoons minced fresh tarragon or 1 1/2 teaspoons
        dried tarragon
1/4 teaspoon salt
Freshly ground pepper

Salad:

1 1/2 pounds unpeeled tiny red new potatoes
2 celery stalks sliced into arcs
1 large red bell pepper, quartered and sliced into strips
1/2 red onion, sliced and separated into rings
1 1/2 tablespoons Dijon mustard
1/4 pound green beans, trimmed and cut in 1 inch pieces
1 6 1/2-ounce can tuna packed in oil
10 oil-cured black olives, halved and pitted
8 cherry tomatoes, halved
3 hard-cooked eggs, peeled and cut into wedges
Minced fresh tarragon or freshly snipped chives

POTATO SALAD NIÇOISE   *continued*

1   Combine dressing ingredients and refrigerate.

2   Slice red potatoes. (a slicing blade on the processer
     does a super job). Place sliced potatoes in a circle
     around edge of a microsafe plate, leaving center
     empty. Cover with plastic wrap and microcook 10-12
     minutes, stirring occasionally. Drain potatoes, rinse
     under cold water and drain again. Pat dry. Place
     potatoes in a large bowl, add dressing and toss. Add
     celery, red pepper, onion and mustard to the potato
     mixture and toss.

3   Wrap green beans in plastic wrap and microcook on
     High Power 2 minutes. Pierce plastic, unwrap care-
     fully, drain, rinse under cold water and drain again.

4   Just before serving, add tuna and green beans to
     potato mixture and toss gently. Adjust seasoning.
     Mound salad on platter. Garnish with olives, cherry
     tomatoes and eggs. Sprinkle with fresh tarragon or
     chives.

Serves 6

The hot dressing on cold, crisp lettuce wedges is a nice change from the usual tossed greens.

LETTUCE WEDGES WITH WARM BLUE CHEESE DRESSING

3 tablespoons grated Parmesan cheese
1 green onion and top, chopped
1 cup mayonnaise
1/2 teaspoon dried basil
1/2 teaspoon prepared horseradish
3 ounces blue cheese
6 wedges iceberg lettuce, well chilled
Paprika

1   Combine Parmesan cheese, chopped onion, mayon-
     naise, basil and horseradish in a microsafe bowl.

2   Crumble blue cheese into mayonnaise mixture and
     microcook on Medium Power (50%) 2 minutes or until
     hot, stirring once after 1 minute. Be careful not to
     overcook as dressing will separate.

3   Spoon dressing over crispy cold lettuce wedges.
     Sprinkle with paprika and serve immediately.

Serves 6

Now that you have mastered cooking bacon in the micro-wave, why not try this tasty salad?

WILTED GREENS SALAD

8 ounces romaine
6 ounces fresh spinach, stems discarded
6 ounces iceberg lettuce
1 medium onion, peeled
8 ounces fresh mushrooms
1/2 pound bacon (cut in 1 inch squares)
1 cup pitted ripe olives
1 6-ounce can water chestnuts

Dressing:

3 tablespoons sugar	2 teaspoons Worcestershire sauce
1/2 cup catsup	1 teaspoon dry mustard
1/2 cup cider vinegar	2 teaspoons salt
4 tablespoons water	1/4 teaspoon pepper

1   Slice romaine, spinach, iceberg lettuce, onion and mushrooms. Use either a sharp knife or the medium slicing blade of the food processor to do the job more quickly.

2   Place bacon in a 3 quart microsafe casserole and microcook on High Power 7-8 minutes or until crisp. Remove bacon. Reserve drippings.

3   Stir sugar, catsup, vinegar, water, Worcestershire sauce, mustard, salt and pepper into bacon drip-pings. Microcook on High Power 4-5 minutes or until boiling.

4   Add sliced greens, ripe olives and water chestnuts to casserole and toss. Sprinkle with bacon and serve immediately.

Serves 8-10

Simply divine and simple to prepare! My friend Diego gave me this recipe and beautiful calamari steaks to make it!

CALAMARI SALAD

3/4-pound medium squid, cleaned and sliced into rings or
    squid steaks cut into narrow strips
3 stalks celery, thinly sliced
1/2 cup thinly sliced yellow onion
1/2 cup thinly sliced red or yellow bell pepper
2 tablespoons olive oil
2 tablespoons fresh lemon juice
1 teaspoon salt
1/4 teaspoon freshly ground black pepper
12 oil-cured black olives, pitted and coarsely chopped

1   Place the squid, celery, onions and bell pepper in a 1
     quart microsafe casserole. Toss ingredients to com-
     bine. Cover with plastic wrap and microcook on
     High Power 2 1/2 minutes, shaking the dish once.

2   Uncover and let cool slightly. Pour off liquid and add
     olive oil, lemon juice, salt, freshly ground black pep-
     per and chopped olives.

3   Serve chilled on a lettuce leaf.

Serves 4

*An interesting combination of wonderful flavors with the
added advantage of being equally delicious hot or cold!*

RAISIN, PECAN AND WILD RICE SALAD

4 cups water
2 cups wild rice
1 cup coarsely chopped pecans
4 tablespoons chopped Italian parsley
1 tablespoon olive oil
Zest of 1 medium orange
Salt and pepper to taste
1/4 cup golden raisins

1   Combine water and rice in a large microsafe casserole. Cover with plastic wrap and microcook on High Power 5-8 minutes or until boiling.

2   Continue to microcook on Medium Power (50%) 15-20 minutes or until the water is absorbed and rice is tender but not mushy. Refrigerate uncovered until cool.

3   When cool combine with the pecans, parsley, olive oil, orange zest, salt, pepper and raisins.

4   Serve chilled or at room temperature. This can also be heated and served as a rice accompaniment to meat. Freezes well.

Serves 6-8

Next time you have leftover french bread, make some of these delicious croutons to add to tossed salads.

GARLIC CROUTONS

1/2 cup butter or margarine
6 sprigs parsley
4 ounces French bread, cut into 1/2 inch cubes
    (about 3 cups)
1 clove garlic, minced

1   Place butter in a large microsafe shallow casserole. Microcook on High Power 1-2 minutes, until melted. Add parsley and minced garlic to butter and mix well.

2   Add bread cubes to butter mixture and toss to coat. Microcook on High Power 3-4 minutes, until lightly browned and dry. Stir once during cooking.

3   Cool to room temperature (croutons become crisper as they cool). Store in airtight container at room temperature up to 1 week or store in freezer up to 2 months. (Hide them from your family as they make wonderful snack food!)

Makes 3 cups

5

SEAFOOD

Scallops with Snow Peas
Coquille St. Jacques
Scallops with Pine Nuts
Fish Filets Amandine
Hot Crab Sandwich
Sherried Crab Crêpes
Poached Salmon with Dill Sauce
Cold Poached Salmon
Tuna Tomato Wedges
Macadamia Sauced Fish Filets
Tarragon Fish Filets in Parchment
Shrimp Scampi

There are wonderful oriental flavors in this fabulous micro-cooked recipe.

SCALLOPS WITH SNOW PEAS

6 medium-size dried shiitake mushrooms
1 green onion, sliced in 1 inch strips lengthwise
3/4 pound scallops, rinsed and patted dry
3 quarter-sized slices fresh ginger
5 teaspoons olive oil
4 teaspoons soy sauce
2 teaspoons dry sherry
1/2 pound snow peas, strings removed and rinsed well

1   Soak mushrooms in hot water 20 minutes. Trim stems from mushrooms and discard. Squeeze to remove most of the moisture and slice into thin slivers.

2   Place remaining onions, mushrooms, scallops, ginger, oil, soy sauce, and sherry in a shallow microsafe casserole. Mix to blend flavors. Cover and let stand at room temperature for 30 minutes. Stir occasionally.

3   Spread scallop mixture in an even layer, cover loosely with waxed paper and microcook on High Power 3-5 minutes or until scallops are opaque. Stir after 2 minutes of cooking. Let mixture stand covered 4-5 minutes.

4   Place snow peas in a microsafe bowl, cover with plastic wrap and microcook on High Power 3-3 1/2 minutes, or until crisp tender. Let stand 1 minute covered.

5   Remove ginger from the scallops and discard. To serve, combine scallops and snow peas and place on side of serving plate. Serve with wild rice.

Serves 2

Though amazingly easy, this classic entrée is fabulous cooked in the microwave. The presentation can be especially elegant if you cook it in large seafood shells.

COQUILLE ST. JACQUES

1 cup sherry
1 bay leaf
1 pound sea scallops
1/2 pound mushrooms, sliced
1/2 medium onion, chopped
1/3 cup butter or margarine
2 tablespoons flour
1 tablespoon lemon juice
1/2 teaspoon salt
Paprika
Pepper
Cayenne pepper
Bread crumbs
Parmesan cheese

1   Place sherry, bay leaf and scallops in a microsafe baking dish. Cover with plastic wrap and microcook on Medium Power (50%) 5-6 minutes or until scallops are tender. Stir once during cooking. Drain liquid and reserve. Cover scallops and let stand.

COQUILLE ST. JACQUES   *continued*

2   Place butter in a microsafe bowl and microcook on
     High Power 1 minute. Add mushrooms and onion to
     the melted butter and microcook on High Power 2-3
     minutes or until onion is tender.

3   Add the reserved wine broth, flour and lemon juice to
     the mushroom mixture. Microcook on High Power 1
     minute, stir and continue to cook until smooth and
     thickened, microcooking in 1 minute intervals.

4   Season the thickened sauce with salt, paprika, pep-
     per and cayenne pepper. Add scallops to the sauce
     and place mixture in a buttered casserole or 4 indi-
     vidual ramekins or large sea shells.

5   Sprinkle with bread crumbs, Parmesan cheese and a
     little paprika. Microcook on High Power 2-3 minutes
     or until bubbly and heated through.

Serves 4

Set the table and light the candles before you cook this wonderful scallop entrée for two!

SCALLOPS WITH PINE NUTS

1/2 pound bay scallops
1/4 cup butter or margarine
3 tablespoons pine nuts
2 green onions, sliced
4 mushrooms, sliced
1 tablespoon lemon juice
1 tablespoon dry sherry
1 clove garlic, minced

1   Rinse scallops and pat dry. Place in 2 seashells or a 1 1/2 quart microsafe casserole.

2   Place butter and pine nuts in a microsafe dish and microcook on High Power 3 minutes, stirring once midway through cooking. Remove nuts and reserve.

3   Add green onions, mushrooms, lemon juice, sherry and garlic to the melted butter remaining after browning the nuts and microcook on High Power 3 minutes.

4   Pour butter-vegetable mixture over scallops and sprinkle with browned pine nuts. Cover loosely with waxed paper and microcook on High Power 4 minutes.

Serves 2

The microwave really knows how to cook seafood. However, you, the computer operator, must remember to follow the timing carefully, as fish cooks very quickly.

FISH FILETS AMANDINE

1 pound fish filets
3 tablespoons lemon juice
3 tablespoons butter or margarine
Seasoned salt
Paprika
1/4 cup slivered almonds

1   Spread the almonds on a microsafe plate. Micro-cook on High Power, 3-6 minutes, checking and stirring after 3 minutes. Continue to cook until they are as brown as you desire.

2   Pat fish filets dry and place in a microsafe shallow baking dish.

3   Place butter in a microsafe bowl or styrofoam cup. Microcook on High Power, 30-45 seconds. Drizzle the butter and lemon juice over the fish.

4   Sprinkle with seasoned salt and paprika, cover loosely with waxed paper and microcook on High Power for 4 1/2 - 5 minutes, or until fish flakes.

5   Garnish with the toasted almonds and serve.

Serves 2-3

My sister-in-law gave me this recipe many years ago. At the end of the recipe she wrote, "Serve to 4 skinny people". Well, I'll leave that up to you!

HOT CRAB SANDWICH

1 6-ounce can crab or 1 cup fresh crab meat
1 cup mayonnaise
2 green onions, entire onion sliced fine
1 cup grated cheddar cheese
4 English muffins

1   Mix crab, mayonnaise, onions and cheese. Spread on halves of 4 English muffins (8 slices).

2   Place 4 slices on a microsafe plate, arranging in a circle. Microcook on High Power, 2-3 minutes, or until bubbly. Cook remaining muffin halves and serve while hot.

Serves: 4

This elegant entrée is sure to impress and delight your guests. The microwave makes it so easy you'll be amazed.

SHERRIED CRAB CRÈPES

2 tablespoons butter or margarine
2 tablespoons flour
1 cup milk
3 tablespoons sherry
1 green onion, chopped
2 tablespoons capers
1/2 teaspoon salt
1 7-ounce can crab, rinsed and drained
1 cup grated cheddar cheese
6 flour tortillas

1   Place the butter in a microsafe dish, microcook on High Power 2 minutes. Add flour and stir to combine. Add milk and microcook on High Power 3 minutes, stirring after 1 1/2 minutes.

2   Add sherry, green onion, capers, salt and crab to the white sauce. Stir to combine.

3   Lay tortillas on counter surface and spoon crab mixture evenly on each tortilla. Roll up and place seam side down in a microsafe rectangular casserole. Sprinkle grated cheddar on top, cover with plastic wrap and microcook on High Power 6-8 minutes or until cheese is melted and crab mixture is heated to serving temperature.

Serves 6

Salmon and dill are inseparable. This is a marvelous entrée to serve with wonderful microcooked fresh vegetables and a green salad.

POACHED SALMON WITH DILL SAUCE

2 medium-size salmon steaks (about 1/2 pound each)
2 green onions, chopped
1 tablespoon lemon juice
2 tablespoons white wine
2 tablespooons butter or margarine
salt and pepper
1/2 cup sour cream
1/2 teaspoon dill weed

1   Place the green onions, lemon juice, white wine and butter in a shallow microsafe baking dish. Microcook on High Power 3-4 minutes or until sauce is boiling and reduced slightly.

2   Place the salmon in the baking dish and spoon the sauce over it. Cover with plastic wrap and microcook on High Power 2 1/2 - 3 minutes, until fish flakes. Check the center to be certain it is cooked. Remove from the oven and let stand covered while making the sauce.

3   Combine the sour cream and dill weed in a micro-safe bowl and microcook on High Power 1-2 minutes, or until heated through.

4   Place the steaks on serving plates and pour sauce over, completely masking them. Serve immediately.

Serves 2

An elegant do-ahead warm weather entrée for elegant dining. Can you believe only 9 minutes cooking time in the microwave? Sauce it with the Dilled Cucumber Sauce (see index) which takes just minutes to prepare, and enjoy your meal with your guests.

COLD POACHED SALMON

4 salmon steaks (about 1/2 pound each)
2 cups water
1/2 lemon, sliced
1/2 onion, sliced
6 whole cloves
1 bay leaf
1 stalk celery, chopped
3 sprigs parsley
1 1/2 teaspoons salt
2 tablespoons lemon juice
3 tablespoons vinegar

1   Combine the water, lemon, onion, cloves, bay leaf, celery, parsley, salt, lemon juice and vinegar in a shallow microsafe dish. Microcook on High Power, uncovered, 5 minutes.

2   Lower the salmon steaks into the hot liquid. Microcook, uncovered on High Power, 4-5 minutes or until salmon flakes slightly. Let salmon cool in the poaching liquid.

3   Lift steaks from the stock, remove skin and bones and chill the steaks for 3 hours.

4   Serve chilled with Cold Cucumber Sauce. (See index for page number)

Serves: 4

No more creamed tuna on rice! Try this one dish dinner soon, it's a great recipe for beginning cooks!

TUNA TOMATO WEDGES

2 eggs
1 1/2 cups cooked rice
6 green onions, chopped
2 7-ounce cans solid oil-packed tuna, undrained
1/2 cup butter or margarine
1/4 teaspoon thyme
1 cup dry bread crumbs
1 large ripe tomato, sliced
3/4 cup grated cheddar cheese

1   Place eggs in a large bowl and beat. Add cooked rice, onions and undrained tuna. Mix well.

2   Place the butter in a microsafe bowl and microcook on High Power for I minute.

3   Add butter, thyme and bread crumbs to tuna-rice mixture. Mix well and spread evenly in a lightly greased 9 inch microsafe pie plate. Cover loosely with waxed paper and microcook on High Power for 9-11 minutes.

4   Arrange tomato slices over top in an overlapping circle, sprinkle grated cheese over all and micro-cook on High Power until cheese is melted, 2-3 minutes.

5   Slice into pie shaped wedges and serve immediately.

Serves 6-8

An unusual combination of flavors creates this wonderful dish.

MACADAMIA SAUCED FISH FILETS

4-6 boneless fish filets, same size and thickness
        (approximately 1 1/2 pounds)
1/4 teaspoon salt
2 teaspoons chopped onion
1 1/2 teaspoons water
3/4 cup mayonnaise
1 teaspoon lemon juice
1/4 teaspoon seasoned salt
1 tablespoon chopped fresh parsley
1 cup chopped macadamia nuts

1   Wipe fillets and sprinkle with salt. Roll fish and secure with wooden picks. Place in a shallow microsafe baking dish and cover loosely with waxed paper. Microcook on High Power 4 minutes or until fish flakes.

2   Combine onion, water, mayonnaise, lemon juice, seasoned salt and parsley in a microsafe bowl. Microcook on Medium Power (50%) 2 minutes, just until heated through. If sauce separates, add a little more lemon juice.

3   Coat the filets with the sauce, sprinkle generously with chopped macadamia nuts and serve immediately.

Serves: 4-6

Not many recipes require ribbon. That's right: ribbon! Any kind of ribbon or even twine will do. The presentation of this wonderful fish entrée is worth a picture. Guests receive their own packages. As they open their surprises, a wonderful lemon-tarragon aroma fills the air and mushroom studded fish filets appear. A FUN entrée for entertaining! Just be certain to provide a large basket or bowl for the parchment and ribbon.

TARRAGON FISH FILETS IN PARCHMENT

1 pound fish filets, 1/2 inch thick (sole, orange roughy etc.;
    1/4 pound for each serving.)
4 teaspoons butter
Salt and pepper
1 tablespoon fresh tarragon, chopped, or 1 teaspoon dried
4 teaspoons lemon juice
4 thin lemon slices
4 sprigs fresh tarragon
8 thick slices fresh mushrooms
Parchment paper
Ribbon or twine

1   Cut 4 12-inch squares of parchment paper. Position each fish filet in the center of a square. Place a teaspoon of butter on each filet, salt and pepper lightly.

TARRAGON FISH FILETS IN PARCHMENT   *continued*

2   Sprinkle each filet with chopped fresh tarragon and 1 teaspoon lemon juice. Fold the filets in half and tuck 2 thick slices of a mushroom in each filet. Top each filet with a lemon slice and a sprig of fresh tarragon.

3   Using both hands, gather up the parchment paper, completely enclosing the fish bundle, and twist the parchment paper two or three times to be certain fish is tightly enclosed. Twist the remaining packages.

4   Now comes the fun. Tie each package with a piece of ribbon, color co-ordinated with your centerpiece, placemats, etc. You may tie them in bows with long streamers, or knot twine around them. Just be creative knowing your guests will be amazed.

5   Place the packages in a circle on a 12 inch round microsafe tray, leaving the center open. Microcook on High Power for 5-7 minutes or until done. To be certain they are done, open a packet and press fish to see if it flakes. Let stand 2 minutes before serving.

Serves 4

Cooking an entrée for 4 in 6 minutes is almost magic. But it works, tastes divine and looks quite beautiful.

SHRIMP SCAMPI

1 pound fresh medium or jumbo shrimp, uncooked
1/2 cup butter or margarine
2 tablespoons lemon juice
2 tablespoons chopped fresh parsley
2 cloves garlic, minced
1/2 teaspoon salt
paprika

1   Shell and devein shrimp.

2   Place butter, lemon juice, parsley, garlic and salt in shallow microsafe casserole. Microcook on High Power for 2 minutes.

3   Add shrimp, stir well and sprinkle with paprika. Microcook on High Power 4-6 minutes, or just until pink and tender, being careful not to overcook.

Serves 3-4

6

POULTRY

Chicken Olé
Turkey Tetrazzini with Almonds
Turkey Piccata for Two
Parmesan Chicken
Five Minute Chicken Dijon for One
Chunky Chicken Curry
Stuffed Chicken Breasts
Chicken Kiev
Teriyaki Chicken
Chicken Tortilla Casserole
Crispy Chicken
Chinese Chicken in Parchment

Here is another microwave recipe that does double duty. Use it as a chicken entrée or roll chicken wing drumettes in the spicy coating and serve as an appetizer.

CHICKEN OLÉ

1 pound chicken thighs, breasts or drumettes
1/2 cup butter or margarine

<u>Taco Seasoning</u>:

2 cups corn flakes	1 teaspoon cumin
2 teaspoons paprika	1 teaspoon onion powder
2 teaspoons chili powder	1/2 teaspoon garlic powder
1 teaspoon salt	1/2 teaspoon dried oregano

1   Combine corn flakes, paprika, chili powder, salt, cumin, onion powder, garlic powder and oregano in a processor or blender container and blend into crumbs.

2   Place butter in a microsafe bowl and microcook 30 seconds or until melted.

3   Dip chicken parts in butter and then roll in taco crumbs.

4   Place chicken parts in a round microsafe pie plate or quiche dish in spoke fashion, with larger part of the chicken piece toward outside of dish.

5   Microcook on High Power 7 minutes per pound or 1 minute per drumette. Serve while warm with plenty of napkins and a "bone dish".

Serves 4-6

This is a recipe you'll want to use with left-over holiday turkey. Prepare it just as soon as you've removed the meat from the carcass and freeze the tetrazzini for later use.

TURKEY TETRAZZINI WITH ALMONDS

1 pound spaghetti, cooked and drained
3 tablespoons butter
1 clove garlic, minced
1 medium onion, chopped
2 tablespoons flour
2 cups chicken broth
1/2 cup milk or cream
2 tablespoons dry vermouth or sherry
1/2 pound fresh mushrooms, sliced
1 teaspoon lemon juice
1/2 teaspoon salt
Freshly ground black pepper
2 cups shredded or diced cooked turkey or chicken
1/2 cup slivered almonds or pine nuts
1 cup grated Parmesan cheese

1   In a large microsafe casserole, combine butter, garlic and onion. Microcook on High Power 1-3 minutes or until onion is tender.

TURKEY TETRAZZINI WITH ALMONDS   *continued*

2   Stir in flour, until dissolved and smooth. Pour in
chicken broth, a little at a time, stirring to keep the
sauce smooth. Add milk or cream and vermouth or
sherry. Microcook on High Power 8-10 minutes or until
boiling, but only slightly thickened, stirring occasionally.

3   Add mushrooms, lemon juice, salt, pepper, turkey,
drained spaghetti, slivered almonds or pine nuts and
1/2 cup Parmesan cheese to the mixture. (If freezing,
stop at this point add cheese on top and wrap in foil
to freeze. To reheat, thaw and continue with recipe.

4   Cover loosely with waxed paper and microcook on
High Power for 10 minutes, stirring after 5 minutes.

5   Sprinkle the remaining 1/2 cup cheese on top and
microcook uncovered on High Power for 4-6 minutes,
or until heated through.

Serves 4-6

Top a mound of rice with a turkey slice, ladle the caper studded sauce over all, toss a green salad and you'll have a lovely piccata dinner for two.

TURKEY PICCATA FOR TWO

2 slices fresh turkey breast meat, pounded thin
1/4 cup vermouth
1 tablespoon lemon juice
2 teaspoons capers, drained
Cornstarch or flour

1   Combine vermouth, lemon juice and capers in a small microsafe casserole.

2   Place turkey breast slices into mixture, cover with plastic wrap and microcook on Medium Power (50%) 2-3 minutes or until turkey slices are no longer pink.

3   Remove turkey slices, cover with foil to keep warm, and thicken sauce with cornstarch or flour if necessary. Microcook sauce on High Power 2 minutes and ladle over turkey slices.

Serves 2

Herbs, cheese and crushed crackers provide a tasty coating for chicken parts. Try this crumb coating on chicken wing drumettes for a crowd pleasing appetizer.

PARMESAN CHICKEN

2 pounds chicken parts
1/2 cup butter or margarine
30 butter crackers
1 cup grated Parmesan cheese
2 tablespoons parsley, chopped
2 teaspoons garlic powder
1 1/2 teaspoons paprika
Freshly ground pepper

1   Place butter in a microsafe dish, and microcook on High Power 30 seconds or until melted.

2   Combine crackers, Parmesan cheese, parsley, garlic powder, paprika and pepper in processor or blender bowl. Process until coarsely crumbed.

3   Dip chicken parts in melted butter to coat, then roll in crumbs. Place chicken pieces in a pie plate or quiche dish in spoke fashion, with meatier part of chicken toward outside of plate.

4   Microcook on High Power 14 minutes, or 7 minutes per pound of chicken.

Serves 6

Be nice to yourself! Fix a little salad, pour a glass of your favorite beverage, put a tape on and then fix your chicken. Relax, and enjoy this fast and fabulous microwave-easy recipe!

FIVE MINUTE CHICKEN DIJON FOR ONE

1 boneless chicken breast half
2 tablespoons mayonnaise or diet mayonnaise
1/2 teaspoon Dijon mustard
1 tablespoon chopped walnuts, pecans or whole pine nuts

1 Place chicken breast half on a microsafe plate, cover with plastic wrap and microcook on High Power 3 minutes. Let stand covered while toasting the nuts and making the sauce.

2 Place nuts on a microsafe plate, microcook on High Power 1 minute or until toasted. Reserve.

3 Combine the mustard and mayonnaise in a small microsafe bowl, microcook on High Power 30 seconds, stir and adjust to your taste.

4 Remove skin from chicken breast and place chicken on a dinner plate. Mask with heated Dijon sauce and sprinkle with toasted chopped nuts.

Serves 1 QUICKLY

(For three servings: 3 boneless chicken breast halves should microcook in 6-7 minutes on High Power. The sauce for three breasts, tripling the ingredients, should microcook in 1-2 minutes on High Power)

This recipe was quite a hit in my cooking classes. It looks elegant when surrounded by the condiments and a bowl of rice.

CHUNKY CHICKEN CURRY

3 chicken breasts
1 tablespoon butter or margarine
1/2 cup chopped onion
1 10-ounce can cream of chicken soup
1/4 cup milk
1-2 tablespoons curry powder
1 cup sour cream
Chutney, coconut, peanuts etc.

1   Place 3 chicken breasts on a microsafe plate, cover with plastic wrap and microcook on High Power 8-10 minutes. Let cool, remove meat from bone and cut into chunks.

2   Place butter and onion in a microsafe bowl, cover with plastic wrap and microcook on High Power 2 minutes.

3   Add soup, milk, curry powder and chicken to butter-onion mixture. Cover with plastic wrap and micro-cook on High Power 5 minutes.

4   Add sour cream, cover with plastic wrap and micro-cook on High Power 2 minutes.

5   Serve over rice and pass condiments to sprinkle over (chopped peanuts, coconut, chutney etc.) See index for Super Simple Perfect Rice and Bengal Chutney recipes.

Serves 4-6

Definitely party fare.

STUFFED CHICKEN BREASTS

4 chicken breasts, halved, skinned and boned (1 1/2
      pounds total)
2 tablespoons chopped green onion
2 tablespoons chopped parsley
1/4 cup sliced water chestnuts or slivered almonds
1/3 pound crabmeat, rinsed, drained and flaked
3 tablespoons butter or margarine
2 teaspoons brandy
2 slices bread, crumbed and microcooked 4 minutes on
      High Power
Salt
Pepper
Paprika

Sauce:

1/2 cup sour cream
1/2 cup mayonnaise
1 teaspoon Dijon Mustard

1   Place chicken breasts between sheets of plastic wrap
      and flatten with meat mallet.

2   Combine sour cream, mayonnaise and Dijon mustard
      in a microsafe bowl. Set aside.

STUFFED CHICKEN BREASTS　　　　　*continued*

3　　Combine onion, parsley, water chestnuts, crab, salt, pepper and 2 tablespoons of the previously prepared sauce. Spoon mixture evenly among the flattened chicken pieces; roll up, tucking in sides. Place the chicken rolls on a microsafe serving platter, placing them in a circle on the outer edge of the platter, seam sides down.

4　　Place butter in a microsafe bowl and microcook on High Power 20 seconds. Stir in brandy. Spoon brandy-butter mixture over chicken. Sprinkle bread crumbs over each breast and pat lightly. Sprinkle with salt, pepper and paprika. Cover loosely with waxed paper and microcook on High Power, 16-18 minutes, or until juices run clear when chicken is pierced with a fork.

5　　Microcook sauce on Medium Power (50%) 3-4 minutes or until hot. Place chicken breasts on dinner plates and ladle sauce over each.

Serves 8

Prepare these chile-stuffed chicken breasts ahead of time, refrigerate and pop into the microwave to cook at the last minute.

CHICKEN KIEV

6 chicken breast halves, boned and skinned
3 tablespoons butter or margarine
1/4 cup grated sharp cheddar cheese
1 tablespoon chopped onion
1 teaspoon salt
2 tablespoons chopped green chiles
6 tablespoons butter
1 cup crushed cheddar cheese crackers

1   Place each chicken breast half between 2 sheets of plastic wrap. Flatten with meat mallet. Remove plastic wrap.

2   Mix together butter, cheese, onion, salt and chiles.

3   Place chicken breast halves on work surface and spoon equal portions of cheese-chile mixture onto each breast half. Roll up each breast, tucking ends in to completely enclose filling. Secure with toothpicks.

CHICKEN KIEV
continued

4   Place butter in a microsafe bowl and melt on High Power 45-60 seconds. Dip each chicken roll in melted butter to coat completely; then cover entirely with cracker crumbs.

5   Arrange chicken in a circle in a large microsafe baking dish. Place the thickest parts of the chicken bundles toward the outside edge of the dish. There should be an empty space in the center of the baking dish. Cover loosely with waxed paper. Microcook on High Power 6-8 minutes. Rearrange chicken bundles and microcook on Medium High Power (70%) 6-8 minutes or until chicken is fork tender.

6   Let stand 5 minutes before removing toothpicks and serving.

Serves 6

Just add rice, a salad and some fruit for dessert and dinner is ready!

TERIYAKI CHICKEN

1/2 cup white wine
1/3 cup soy sauce
3 tablespoons honey
3 pounds chicken parts
1 8-ounce can sliced water chestnuts
2 tablespoons water
1 1/2 tablespoons cornstarch

1   Combine wine, soy sauce, honey and chicken parts in a plastic bag. Marinate 1 hour, turning bag to mix contents.

2   Place chicken parts, marinade and water chestnuts in a microsafe casserole and microcook on High Power 9-12 minutes.

3   Rearrange chicken parts and microcook on High Power for another 9-12 minutes or until done. Test for doneness by piercing with a fork. Juices should run clear, not pink.

4   Place chicken on a serving platter. Cover with foil to keep warm.

5   Combine water and cornstarch, stir into pan juices and microcook on High Power 2-3 minute or until thickened. Stir occasionally during cooking. Pour over chicken and serve.

Serves 4

Another "fix ahead, freeze and microcook it later" casse-role.

CHICKEN TORTILLA CASSEROLE

1 dozen medium size corn tortillas, cut into quarters
5 large chicken breasts
1 10-ounce can cream of mushroom soup
1 10-ounce can cream of chicken soup
3/4 cup half and half
2 7-ounce cans green chile salsa
1 onion, chopped
1 can sliced ripe olives, drained
1/2 pound grated cheddar cheese, divided

1   Place chicken breasts on a large microsafe platter, placing meatier parts toward outer edge of platter. Cover with plastic wrap and microcook 6-8 minutes per pound, turning pieces over mid way through cooking. If juices run clear when chicken is pierced with a fork, chicken is cooked. Cover with plastic wrap and let stand 5 minutes.

2   When cool, remove skin and chunk chicken, saving broth. Place 1/4 cup reserved broth in a 9 x 13 microsafe shallow casserole. Layer tortillas over broth and scatter chicken chunks over tortillas.

3   Combine the 2 soups, half and half, onion, salsa, drained olives and 1/2 the grated cheddar. Spread over chicken layer and microcook, covered with plastic wrap, on High Power 12-14 minutes or until bubbly and hot. (An instant read thermometer check should be at least 160 degrees.)

4   Sprinkle with remaining cheese, cover with plastic wrap and let stand 3-5 minutes before serving.

Serves 8-10

Crispy chicken in the microwave? Yes, and you don't use butter or oil.

CRISPY CHICKEN

1 cup crushed cornflakes
4 chicken breasts, 1-1 1/2 pounds, bone in
1 tablespoon garlic salt or other seasonings
1/3 cup evaporated milk

1   Combine crumbs and garlic salt.

2   Dip chicken in evaporated milk and roll in seasoned crumbs.

3   Place chicken in microsafe casserole with meatier part of pieces on outer edge of casserole. Cover loosely with waxed paper and microcook on High Power 10-12 minutes. Let stand 3 minutes, loosely covered with wax paper.

Serves 4

These special packages will be the hit of your next Chinese dinner party! They are easy to prepare ahead of time. Keep them in your refrigerator, microcook them at the last minute and surprise your guests with a bow-tied package for each.

CHINESE CHICKEN IN PARCHMENT

8 boneless, skinless chicken breasts (note total weight of
    chicken)
8 fresh mushrooms, sliced
24 snow peas
16 chunks canned pineapple
16 tablespoons bottled plum sauce
Ribbon or twine
8 squares parchment paper

1   Place chicken breasts on parchment squares.

2   Sprinkle mushroom slices, pea pods and pineapple chunks over chicken breasts and drizzle each stack with 2 tablespoons plum sauce.

3   Fold to seal into a package or twist into a pouch and tie with twine or ribbon. Arrange packages in a circle on a microsafe platter. Microcook on High Power 7-8 minutes per pound of chicken.

Serves 8

7

MEAT

Herbed Beef with Polenta
Teriyaki Skewers
"Souper" Fast Beef Stroganoff
Beef and Noodles
Mexican Lasagne
Simplified Tacos
Hamburger Stroganoff
Lamb Moussaka
Reuben Casserole
Ham and Cheese Crèpes
Pork Tenderloin with Madeira Sauce
Pork Chops with Pasta

Polenta combines with beef strips for a nice main dish fit for family or friends. These tomato sauced servings go well with a green salad or a vegetable.

HERBED BEEF WITH POLENTA

1 pound top round steak
1/4 cup chopped onion
1 tablespoon flour
1/2 cup sliced ripe olives
2 teaspoons chili powder
1/2 teaspoon salt
1 8-ounce can tomato sauce
1 cup yellow cornmeal

3/4 cup milk
1 cup water
1/2 teaspoon marjoram
1/2 teaspoon oregano
3/4 teaspoon salt
2 tablespoons butter or
  margarine
Grated Parmesan cheese

1   Slice beef thinly across grain into narrow strips. Cut strips into 1/2 inch pieces.

2   Combine beef, onion, flour, olives, chili powder, 1/2 teaspoon salt and 1/2 can tomato sauce in a 9 inch microsafe pie plate. Microcook on High Power 5 minutes, stirring twice during cooking. Cover with plastic wrap and let stand.

3   Combine cornmeal, milk, water, marjoram, oregano and 3/4 teaspoon salt in a microsafe bowl. Microcook on High Power 4-5 minutes, stirring well 2-3 times during cooking. Cook just until smooth and thick but not dry. Stir in butter and spoon over the beef mixture.

4   Spoon remaining 1/2 can tomato sauce over top, sprinkle lightly with Parmesan cheese and microcook on High Power 2-4 minutes or until hot.

Serves 4-6

These colorful, low calorie vegetable-beef skewers are cooked in a most interesting way. The flavor from the marinade is outstanding.

TERIYAKI SKEWERS

1 1/2 pounds sirloin steak, 1/2 inch thick
1 clove garlic, minced
1 tablespoon fresh ginger, chopped
1/2 cup soy sauce
1 teaspoon sugar
1 small onion, chopped
8 whole fresh mushrooms
8 green pepper slices
8 cherry tomatoes
8 12-inch bamboo skewers

1   Cut steak across the grain into long, 1/4 inch wide strips.

2   Combine garlic, ginger, soy sauce, sugar and onion.

3   Marinate the steak strips for 30 minutes to 1 hour. (Do not marinate longer than 2 hours as the flavors get too strong.)

4   Lace steak strips in an "S" type fashion onto wooden skewers. Atlernate curves of the "S" with a mushroom, then a green pepper slice and a cherry tomato on the end.

5   Place skewers across a 9" x 12" rectangular microsafe casserole, with ends of skewers resting on top edges of casserole. Microcook on High Power 4 minutes, turn, baste with marinade, and microcook 3 minutes on second side.

Serves 4 (2 skewers per person)

Keep these ingredients on hand for a fast and fabulous dinner.

"SOUPER" FAST BEEF STROGANOFF

3 tablespoons butter or margarine
1 pound beef round steak
2/3 cup water
1 3-ounce can mushroom slices with liquid (or 2/3 cup fresh
        mushrooms sautéed in 2 tablespoons butter)
1 envelope dry onion soup mix
1 cup sour cream
2 tablespoons flour
2 tablespoons catsup
1/4 teaspoon garlic powder

1   Trim fat from meat and cut meat diagonally across
     the grain in very thin strips. Place butter in a micro-
     safe shallow dish and microcook on High Power 30-45
     seconds. Add meat and cook on High Power 3
     minutes.

2   Add water, mushrooms and soup mix to the meat
     and stir to blend. Microcook on High Power 4-6
     minutes, or until bubbling.

3   Mix the flour into the sour cream and add to the hot
     meat-soup mixture. Add the catsup and garlic
     powder. Microcook on Medium High Power (70%)
     until mixture thickens. Do not overcook as meat will
     toughen.

4   Serve over rice or noodles.

Serves 4-6

Here is a fast and delicious one-dish dinner for family or a crowd.

BEEF AND NOODLES

1 pound ground beef
1 14 1/2-ounce can stewed tomatoes, undrained
1 8-ounce can tomato sauce
2 teaspoons salt
2 teaspoons sugar
2 cloves garlic, minced
1 12-ounce package egg noodles, cooked
1 3-ounce package cream cheese
1 cup sour cream
6 green onions sliced (including tops)
1 cup grated sharp cheddar cheese

1   Place ground beef in microsafe bowl and microcook on High Power 3-5 minutes, stirring every minute to avoid lumps. Drain grease from meat. If you have a microsafe colander proceed as above, using a plate under the colander to catch the grease. Stir occasionally. (This method prevents hard lumps from forming, as the grease is drained off as meat is cooked.) Add stewed tomatoes, tomato sauce, salt, sugar and garlic. Cover with plastic wrap and microcook on Medium Power (50%) 5-6 minutes.

BEEF AND NOODLES   *continued*

2   Combine the cooked, drained noodles with cream
         cheese, sour cream and green onions.

3   Remove half the meat-tomato mixture from the
         casserole and reserve. Layer 1/2 the noodle mixture
         on top ot the beef mixture remaining in the casserole.
         Layer the remaining meat sauce over the noodles,
         and spread the remaining noodles over this layer.

4   Cover with plastic wrap and microcook on High
         Power 8-9 minutes or until bubbly and center is hot.
         Sprinkle with grated cheddar cheese. Re-cover with
         plastic wrap and let stand 3 minutes before serving.

Serves 6-8

This is a cooking class favorite. Tortillas come to the rescue again and combine nicely with beef, cheese and spices.

MEXICAN LASAGNE

1 pound ground beef
1 8-ounce can tomato sauce
1 1.25-ounce package taco seasoning mix
8-ounces ricotta cheese
2 green onions, chopped, including green part
2 tablespoons diced chiles
1 egg
1 6-ounce package mozzarella cheese, sliced
3 medium-size flour tortillas, quartered
1 cup grated cheddar cheese

1   Place ground beef in a microsafe colander on a plate, or use a microsafe bowl. Microcook on High Power 4-5 minutes or until no longer pink. Be certain to stir every minute while cooking to avoid hard lumps. Drain grease. (It's better to use the colander because grease drains off while meat is cooking, thus preventing hard lumps from forming.)

2   Combine meat with tomato sauce and taco seasoning.

MEXICAN LASAGNE   *continued*

3   Combine ricotta cheese, green onions, chiles and egg.

4   Layer half of the meat mixture in bottom of a 2 quart casserole. Place mozzarella slices over meat layer. Spread ricotta mixture over cheese slices. Scatter tortilla pieces over ricotta layer and top with remaining meat mixture.

5   Cover with plastic wrap and microcook on High Power 9 minutes. Remove plastic wrap and sprinkle cheddar cheese over top. Recover with plastic wrap and let stand 5 minutes or until cheese is melted. Reheat on Medium Power (50%) 5 minutes if necessary.

Serves 6-8

Taco lovers will go for this combination. It makes a nice presentation as the star of a buffet dinner.

SIMPLIFIED TACOS

1 pound lean ground beef
1 medium onion, chopped
1 6-ounce can tomato paste
1 1 1/4-ounce package taco seasoning mix
1 1/2 cups water
1 16-ounce package taco chips
2 cups grated sharp cheddar cheese
1 avocado, diced
1 cup sour cream
2 tomatoes, diced
1/2 head iceberg lettuce, thinly sliced
1 2 1/4-ounce can sliced ripe olives

1   Place the ground beef and chopped onion in a microsafe casserole. Mix well and microcook on High Power 3 minutes, stir and cook 3 minutes longer. Drain grease.

2   Add tomato paste, taco seasoning mix and water to meat mixture. Microcook on High Power 4 minutes, stir, cook 4 minutes longer.

3   Pour sauce over the taco chips and let guests serve themselves, adding toppings of cheese, avocado, sour cream, tomato, lettuce and olives.

4   The sauce-chip mixture can be easily reheated by microcooking on High Power 3-4 minutes.

Serves 4-6

Here is another recipe that can be served several ways. You might spoon it over hot cooked noodles or ladle it into hot baked potatoes for dinner in a potato.

HAMBURGER STROGANOFF

1 pound ground beef
2 tablespoons flour
1 cup water
1 cup sour cream
3 tablespoons dry onion soup mix
1/2 pound fresh mushrooms, sliced
1/4 teaspoon garlic salt
Pepper
Chopped parsley for garnish

1   Place meat in microsafe dish, microcook on High Power 4 minutes, stirring every minute to prevent lumps. Drain grease. Or cook using colander method (see 101 Quick Tricks, Beef-Cooking).

2   Add flour and water to beef and microcook, on High Power 3-4 minutes, stirring every minute.

3   Add sour cream, mushrooms, onion soup, garlic salt and pepper to thickened beef mixture. Microcook on Medium Power (50%) 5 minutes, being careful not to boil. Serve over noodles or rice.

Serves 4-6

Your microwave really simplifies preparation of this flavorful dish.

LAMB MOUSSAKA

1 small eggplant (3/4-1 pound)
1 medium onion, chopped
1 clove garlic, minced
1 pound lean ground lamb
1 teaspoon salt
1/2 teaspoon cinnamon
1 medium tomato, thinly sliced
3 tablespoons butter or margarine
3 tablespoons flour
1 1/2 cups milk
1/2 cup grated Parmesan cheese
1/8 teaspoon white pepper
1 egg yolk

1   Cut eggplant into 1/2 inch cubes. Combine with onion and garlic in a 2 quart microsafe baking dish. Cover with plastic wrap and microcook on High Power 12 minutes, stirring twice.

2   Combine lamb, salt and cinnamon in a microsafe shallow dish. Microcook on High Power 4 minutes, stirring twice. Drain grease.

LAMB MOUSSAKA   *continued*

3   Remove half of the eggplant mixture from the baking
        dish and reserve. Cover eggplant in baking dish with
        the cooked lamb. Layer with remaining eggplant
        and top with tomato slices.

4   For sauce, combine butter and flour in a 1 quart
        microsafe bowl. Microcook on High 1 minute. Stir in
        milk, Parmesan cheese and white pepper. Micro-
        cook on High Power 4 minutes, stirring twice. Beat in
        egg yolk.

5   Pour sauce over tomato topped lamb-eggplant
        mixture and microcook on High Power 5-6 minutes or
        until hot.

Serves 4-6

Those wonderful flavors of a Reuben sandwich, combine to make an unusual casserole.

REUBEN CASSEROLE

1 16-ounce can sauerkraut, drained
3/4 pound corned beef, broken in pieces
2 cups shredded Swiss cheese
1/2 cup mayonnaise
1/4 cup bottled Thousand Island dressing
2 medium tomatoes, sliced
2 tablespoons butter or margarine
2 slices pumpernickel bread, crumbed

1   Place sauerkraut in 1 1/2 quart microsafe baking dish. Top with pieces of corned beef and shredded cheese.

2   Combine mayonnaise and salad dressing and pour over corned beef-cheese mixture. Layer tomato slices over the top.

3   Place butter in a microsafe bowl and microcook on High Power 30 seconds. Stir in bread crumbs and sprinkle over top.

4   Microcook the casserole on High Power 12-14 minutes until heated through or a microsafe instant read thermometer registers 150 degrees.

Serves 4-6

Flour tortillas make fantastic wrappers for this easy to fix main course topped with a sherry-cheese sauce.

HAM AND CHEESE CRÈPES

10 medium size flour tortillas
10 thin slices ham (packaged rectangular slices are fine)
1 4-ounce can chopped green chiles
1/2 pound grated Monterey Jack cheese
1 10 3/4-ounce can cheddar cheese soup
1/2 cup mayonnaise
2 tablespoons sherry
2 whole green onions, thinly sliced, for garnish

1 Place individual tortillas on work surface. Place ham slice on each and generously sprinkle the chopped chiles and grated cheese over the ham.

2 Roll up each tortilla-crèpe and place seam side down in a 9 x 13 microsafe casserole.

3 Combine cheddar cheese soup, mayonnaise and sherry in a microsafe bowl. Microcook on High Power for 2 minutes.

4 Pour sauce over the crepes, cover with plastic wrap and microcook on High Power 11-12 minutes, or until heated through. Garnish with sliced green onions and serve.

Serves 5-10

The even shape of a pork tenderloin makes it a wonderful candidate for microwave cooking. This tender meat with its flavorful sauce is truly company fare. Start microcooking the pork while your guests enjoy the first course.

PORK TENDERLOIN WITH MADEIRA SAUCE

1 pork tenderloin (to be cooked, just before serving)

Brown Sauce:
4 tablespoons butter or margarine
1 small onion, finely chopped
1 stalk celery, finely chopped
1 carrot, peeled and finely chopped
3 tablespoons flour
1 tomato, peeled, seeded and finely chopped
2 tablespoons tomato puree
3 cups beef stock
1/4 cup dry sherry
1 bay leaf
Parsley sprigs
Salt
Freshly ground pepper

Madeira Sauce:

1/2 pound fresh mushrooms, sliced
4 tablespoons butter or margarine
2 cups brown sauce
1/2 cup Madeira wine
1 tablespoon brandy

1   Place butter for brown sauce in a microsafe bowl. Microcook on High Power 30 seconds. Add onion, celery and carrot and microcook on High Power, 5 minutes.

PORK TENDERLOIN WITH MADEIRA SAUCE   *continued*

2   Stir in flour and microcook on High Power 1 minute.
Add tomato, tomato purée, beef stock, sherry, bay
leaf, parsley, salt and pepper. Microcook on Medium
Power for 30 minutes, stirring occasionally and cooking until sauce is reduced to 3-3 1/2 cups.

3   Remove bay leaf and pour sauce into processor bowl
fitted with steel blade. Process until smooth.

4   In another microsafe bowl, melt 4 tablespoon butter
on High Power 30 seconds. Add sliced mushrooms
and microcook on High Power 3-5 minutes.

5   Add 2 cups of the previously made brown sauce and
microcook on High Power 5-6 minutes, or until boiling.
Stir in Madeira and brandy. Microcook on High
Power 4-5 minutes. Microcook on Medium Power
(50%) for 5 minutes. Taste and adjust seasonings.

6   Microcook pork tenderloin on High Power 8-9 minutes
per pound. Let stand covered 3-5 minutes.

7   Slice pork tenderloin, reheat sauce if necessary and
ladle over individual servings. Garnish with parsley.

8   Remaining brown sauce may be frozen and used as
base for another sauce.

Serves 4

These tender chops are ready in no time, thanks to pre-pared spaghetti sauce and your microwave.

PORK CHOPS AND PASTA

6 pork chops (about 2 pounds)
1 cup prepared spaghetti sauce
1/4 pound fresh mushrooms, sliced
1 tablespoon olive oil
3 large cloves garlic, minced
2 tablespoons chopped parsley
1/2 teaspoon dried Italian herbs or thyme
Pinch salt
Freshly gound black pepper
8 ounces fresh pasta

1   Arrange chops in a 12 inch square microsafe baking dish, placing bony sides against sides of dish.

2   Combine spaghetti sauce, mushrooms, olive oil, garlic, parsley and herbs. Spoon over chops. Cover tightly with plastic wrap. Microcook on High Power 8 minutes. (an instant read thermometer should read 145 F). Let chops stand covered.

3   Prepare pasta as package directs. To serve place a mound of hot pasta on each plate and top each mound with 2 pork chops. Ladle sauce over chops and pasta.

Serves 3

8

VEGETABLES

Spaghetti Squash with White Clam Sauce
Eggplant Parmesan Diet Snack
Tomato Mozzarella Melts
Colorful Carrots
Artichokes
Dilled Zucchini and Mushrooms
Cheese Frosted Cauliflower
Glazed Broccoli with Almonds
Vegetable Medley
Potatoes Romanoff
Potatoes Anna
Taco Topped Baked Potatoes
Low-Cal Cottage Cheese Topped Potatoes
Dilled Oil and Vinegar Potato Topping

Discover the nutty flavor of this magical squash that actually looks like pasta. Cooking it in the microwave saves much time. Add the white clam sauce and you have a fantastic entrée. It's low in calories and has the added advantage of tasting wonderful hot or cold.

SPAGHETTI SQUASH WITH WHITE CLAM SAUCE

1 large spaghetti squash (about 3 pounds)
1 6-ounce can whole clams   1/3 cup white wine
1/4 cup olive oil   3-4 cloves minced garlic
Freshly ground pepper   1/4 cup chopped parsley

1   With a pointed knife, pierce the squash in several places. Microcook squash on High Power 15 minutes (5 minutes per pound).

2   Let stand ten minutes to cool. Cut open the squash lengthwise, remove seeds and with a fork, comb the squash flesh. Place the resulting spaghetti strands in a bowl and cover with plastic wrap.

3   Pour olive oil in a microsafe bowl with minced garlic. Microcook on High Power 3-5 minutes, or until garlic is cooked but not brown. Add broth from canned clams, wine and pepper to cooked garlic and oil. Microcook on High Power 4-5 minutes or until boiling.

4   Add clams to sauce and simmer 2 minutes on Medium Power (50%) or until clams are just heated through. Do not overcook as clams will toughen. Pour sauce over the hot spaghetti squash and toss with chopped parsley. Season with additional salt and pepper to taste. Serve immediately.

5   You can vary this recipe by serving the squash with a garlic butter or marinara sauce.

Serves 6-8

Here is an elegant, low calorie vegetable snack that is quickly prepared in your microwave.

EGGPLANT PARMIGIANA DIET SNACK

1/2 cup diet mayonnaise
2 slices eggplant, 1/2 inch thick
2 tablespoons Parmesan cheese
1 teaspoon oregano
4 tablespoons diet marinara sauce
2 tomato slices
2 slices Monterey jack cheese

1.   Spread both sides of eggplant slices with mayon-
       naise. Place slices in a microsafe baking dish.
       Sprinkle with Parmesan cheese and oregano.

2   Sauce each slice with 2 tablespoons marinara sauce.

3   Top each eggplant stack with a tomato slice and a
       slice of Monterey jack cheese. Microcook on High
       Power 3-4 minutes or until bubbly.

Serves 1

The fresh and special ingredients in this recipe make a nice first course or lunch for two.

TOMATO MOZZARELLA MELTS

2 thick slices tomato
2 thick slices mozzarella cheese (best quality you can buy,
    or Italian Buffalo, if available)
2 teaspoons virgin olive oil
1 teaspoon chopped fresh basil leaves (or sprinkling of
    dried Italian herbs)

1   Place tomato slices on a microsafe plate, cover each
    with a cheese slice.

2   Drizzle olive oil over each and sprinkle with herbs.
    Microcook on High Power 1-2 minutes just until
    cheese begins to bubble and melt.

Serves 2

Brown sugar and dates sweeten colorful carrots. Shredding rather than slicing the carrots adds a more appealing texture as well. Now your kids will eat them!

COLORFUL CARROTS

2 cups shredded carrots
1/3 cup butter or margarine
1/3 cup brown sugar
3/4 cup chopped dates
1/4 teaspoon salt

1   Place butter in microsafe casserole and microcook on High Power 30 seconds.

2   Add carrots, brown sugar, dates and salt. Mix well, cover with plastic wrap and microcook on High Power 4-6 minutes.

Serves 4

If you have had trouble cooking artichokes in the micro-wave, try this method. It is quick and easy.

ARTICHOKES

4 artichokes
1 clove garlic, cut in half
4 lemon slices
4 tablespoons olive oil

1   Trim prickly points off leaves and cut stem. Place artichokes in a circle in a round microsafe casserole, stem end up. Add water to cover 1/3 of the arti-choke.

2   Place the lemon slices around the artichokes, add the garlic pieces to the water and drizzle 1 table-spoon olive oil over each artichoke. Cover with plastic wrap and microcook on High Power for 16 minutes or until stems are fork tender. Immediately turn artichokes upside down, stem end down, and recover with plastic wrap.

3   Let stand 5 minutes. Drain and serve. Or drain and refrigerate. Serve chilled with homemade mayon-naise as a dipping sauce.

Serves 4

This easy recipe transforms zucchini into a company dish.

DILLED ZUCCHINI AND MUSHROOMS

4 medium zucchini, cut in 1 inch slices
1/4 cup water
1/4 teaspoon dried dill weed
1 clove garlic
1/4 cup butter or margarine
1/2 pound mushrooms, sliced
2 tablespoons flour
1 cup sour cream

1   Combine zucchini, water, dill weed and garlic in a 2 quart microsafe casserole. Cover with plastic wrap and microcook on High Power 8 minutes, stirring twice. Let stand covered while making sauce.

2   Place butter and mushrooms in a 2 quart microsafe bowl and microcook on High Power 2 minutes, stirring once.

3   Drain the zucchini, reserving 2 tablespoons of the liquid. Discard garlic clove. Add flour to the mushrooms along with the reserved liquid. Stir and microcook on High Power 1 minute.

4   Spoon zucchini into the mushroom mixture and microcook on High Power 1 minute. Fold in the sour cream and microcook on High Power 2 minutes or until heated through.

Serves 5-6

This makes a beautiful, colorful addition to any buffet dinner.

CHEESE FROSTED CAULIFLOWER

1 medium head cauliflower, trimmed and cored
1/2 cup chicken broth
1/2 cup mayonnaise
1/2 teaspoon prepared mustard
1 whole green onion, chopped
1 cup grated cheddar cheese

1   Place cauliflower and chicken broth in microsafe pie plate. Cover with plastic wrap and microcook on High Power 6-9 minutes, or until cauliflower is easily pierced with a fork.

2   Combine mayonnaise, mustard and green onion. Spread mixture evenly over cauliflower. Press grated cheese into the sauce. Microcook on High Power 1-2 minutes or until cheese begins to melt.

Serves 6-8

There is nothing more beautiful than fresh vegetables cooked in the microwave. The bright green broccoli in this recipe combines well with the sherry-cheese white sauce. Your dinner guests will love it.

GLAZED BROCCOLI WITH ALMONDS

2 pounds broccoli spears or 2 10-ounce packages frozen
     spears
1/2 teaspoon salt
4 tablespoons butter or margarine
4 tablespoons flour
1 cup cream
1 bouillon cube
3/4 cup hot water
2 tablespoons sherry
2 tablespoons lemon juice
1 cup grated cheddar or 1/4 cup Parmesan cheese
1/4 cup slivered almonds

1   Place rinsed broccoli spears in a 9 x 12 microsafe casserole, cover with plastic wrap and microcook on High Power 10-12 minutes or until just tender. Let stand covered while making the sherried cream sauce.

GLAZED BROCCOLI WITH ALMONDS   *continued*

2   In microsafe bowl, combine salt, butter and flour. Microcook on High Power 1 minute, stir well. Add cream and a bouillon cube that has been dissolved in hot water. (To speed dissolving of the bouillon cube, microcook on High Power 1 minute.) Stir well. Add sherry and lemon juice. Microcook on High Power 4-5 minutes or until sauce is thickened and smooth.

3   Spread slivered almonds on a microsafe plate and microcook on High Power 3-5 minutes or until lightly toasted.

4   Drain the cooked broccoli and pour the sauce over the spears. Sprinkle grated cheese and toasted slivered almonds over top. Microcook on High Power 5-7 minutes or until cheese melts and sauce is bubbly.

Serves 6-8

This easy yet beautiful vegetable platter always brings 'ohs and ahs' from guests. It has it all: fast, fabulous, colorful in presentation and it tastes divine.

VEGETABLE MEDLEY

2 bunches broccoli, stalks removed
1 small cauliflower, cut in flowerets
1 large zucchini, sliced
1 large crookneck squash, sliced
6 medium fresh mushrooms, sliced
1 red pepper, cut into strips
1 medium green pepper, cut into strips
1/4 cup butter or margarine
1/2 teaspoon garlic salt
1/4 teaspoon pepper
1/4 teaspoon dry mustard

1   If possible, weigh prepared vegetables for most accurate cooking. Determine total weight and apply to cooking time in step 4 below.

2   Arrange broccoli around outside edge of a large microsafe serving platter that will fit in your microwave oven. Arrange cauliflower in a circle inside the broccoli ring. Arrange zucchini, squash, mushrooms, red pepper and green pepper inside the circle to distribute color for most attractive presentation.

VEGETABLE MEDLEY   *continued*

3   Combine butter, garlic salt, pepper and mustard in a
         microsafe bowl. Microcook on High Power 30-45
         seconds to melt butter.

4   Drizzle butter over vegetables, cover with plastic
         wrap and microcook on High Power 6-7 minutes per
         pound of vegetables. If you are unable to weigh the
         vegetables, microcook on High Power 10-12 minutes
         or until vegetables are tender crisp. Rotate dish once
         during cooking. Let stand, covered, 5 minutes before
         serving.

Serves 10-12

A lovely, make ahead potato casserole for your next dinner party. Your microwave cuts the preparation time and the cooking time down to just minutes.

POTATOES ROMANOFF

6 medium-size baking potatoes, unpeeled
2 cups grated cheddar cheese
1/4 cup butter or margarine
2 cups sour cream
1/4 cup sliced green onion (including green part)
1 teaspoon salt
1/4 teaspoon pepper

1   Wash and pierce potatoes. Microcook on High Power 13-15 minutes or until barely tender. Set aside to cool.

2   Place 1 1/2 cups grated cheese and butter in large microsafe bowl. Microcook on Medium High Power (70%), 2 minutes, or until melted. Stir in sour cream, green onions, salt and pepper.

3   Peel potatoes and grate using grating blade of processor or hand grater. Stir into cheese mixture and spoon into a 2 quart microproof baking dish. If you are planning to serve this casserole at a later time, prepare to this stage, cover with plastic wrap and refrigerate 1-2 days.

4   Smooth top and microcook on Medium High Power (70%) 7-9 minutes or until warm in center.

5   Sprinkle remaining 1/2 cup cheese on top and microcook on High Power 1-2 minutes, or until cheese is melted.

Serves 4-6

A fast potato dish that looks and tastes divine.

POTATOES ANNA

1 1/2 pounds potatoes, peeled
1/2 cup butter or margarine
1 teaspoon paprika
1/2 cup Parmesan cheese, grated

1   Slice the potatoes paper thin (the thinnest slicing disk of the food processor does a beautiful job of slicing, or use a hand held potato peeler). To prevent discoloring, place the slices in a bowl of cold water until ready to cook.

2   Place the butter in a microsafe bowl and microcook on High Power for 1 minute.

3   Pour half the butter into a microsafe oval casserole and lightly sprinkle with cheese and paprika. Carefully layer the potato slices circling the dish and filling the middle. Pour over the remaining butter and microcook on High for 10-12 minutes.

4   Pour off excess butter, loosen edges of potatoes and invert on a serving platter. Serve immediately.

Serves 6

Here's "dinner in a potato". Your family will love this special treat. You can serve the potatoes with a variety of toppings and a salad as a casual buffet. Your microwave makes it fast and fabulous with little effort from you.

TACO TOPPED BAKED POTATOES

1 pound lean ground beef
1/2 cup chopped onion
1/4 cup chopped green pepper
1 8-ounce can tomato sauce
3 tablespoons chopped canned green chiles
1 teaspoon salt
3/4 cup shredded sharp cheddar cheese
3/4 cup dairy sour cream
Diced tomatoes
Shredded lettuce
4 microcooked baking potatoes

1   Place beef, onion and green pepper in a medium size microsafe bowl and microcook on High Power, 7-9 minutes. Be certain to stir every 2 minutes, cooking until meat is no longer pink and vegetables are tender. Drain off fat. For an easier cooking method, see 101 Quick Tricks, ground beef, cooking. This method uses a colander for more even grease free cooking.

2   Stir in tomato sauce, chiles and salt, blending well.

3   Just before serving, slash tops of 4 hot, microcooked potatoes and put a quarter of the cheese and a quarter of the sour cream into each baked potato.

4   Reheat meat sauce by microcooking on High Power 1-2 minutes. Pour over cheese and sour cream and garnish with diced tomatoes and shredded lettuce. Microcook each taco topped potato on High Power 1 minute and serve.

Serves 4

A vegetarian entrée that is quite colorful as well as being low in calories.

LOW-CAL COTTAGE CHEESE TOPPED POTATOES

2 cups small curd, low-fat cottage cheese
1/2 cup grated carrot
1/4 cup sliced radish
1/4 cup chopped green pepper
1/4 cup sliced green onion, including green part
1/4 teaspoon salt or seasoned salt
1/4 teaspoon black pepper
4 medium size baking potatoes, microcooked

1   Place cottage cheese in a medium size microsafe
     bowl. Microcook on Low Power (30%) 3-4 minutes,
     stirring every minute, until just warmed to room tem-
     perature. Do not over-heat. Stir in carrots, radishes,
     green peppers, green onion, salt and pepper, mixing
     well.

2   Spoon evenly over split tops of 4 hot microcooked
     potatoes.

Serves 4

This easy potato topping is a nice change from the usual butter, sour cream and chives and is lower in calories too.

DILLED OIL AND VINEGAR POTATO TOPPING

3/4 cup olive oil
1/2 cup chopped green onions (including the green parts)
1/3 cup red wine vinegar
1/2 cup chopped dill pickle
1/2 teaspoon dried dill weed
1/2 teaspoon salt
1/8 teaspoon freshly ground pepper

1   Place 1 tablespoon olive oil and green onions in a microsafe bowl. Microcook uncovered, on High Power 2 minutes, or until slightly softened.

2   Add remaining olive oil, vinegar, chopped pickle, dill weed, salt and pepper, blending well. Spoon into hot microcooked baking potatoes which have been split open.

Makes 1 1/2 cups

9

GRAINS AND PASTA

Polenta with Cheese and Mushrooms
Mushroom, Spinach and Goat Cheese Lasagne
Super Simple Perfect Rice (Plus 4 Variations)
Fast and Fabulous Rice Casserole
Tex-Mex Rice
Rice Pilaf
Chile Cheese Rice Casserole
Spinach Lasagne Rolls
Pine Nut Vegetable Pilaf

My grandfather, who lived to be 101 years old, called this 'mush'. Today every fancy restaurant in San Francisco serves it and calls it polenta. Now you can make it quickly and easily in the microwave and call it anything you wish.

POLENTA WITH CHEESE AND MUSHROOMS

1/4 pound fresh mushrooms, sliced
1 medium onion, chopped
1/4 cup butter or margarine
3 cups water
1 cup coarse ground yellow cornmeal
1/2 teaspoon salt
4 sprigs parsley, chopped
2 ounces Parmesan cheese, grated

1   Place mushrooms, onions and 2 tablespoons of butter in a microsafe bowl. Cover with plastic wrap and microcook on High Power until onion is tender, 4-5 minutes.

2   Microcook water in a microsafe loaf pan (8 1/2" x 4 1/2" x 2 1/2") on High Power, until simmering. Add cornmeal and salt gradually, stirring continuously. Microcook uncovered on High Power until mixture boils and thickens, 3-5 minutes, stirring after 1 1/2 minutes. Let boil 1 minute.

3   Stir in onion-mushroom mixture, cheese, parsley, and remaining 2 tablespoons of butter. Let stand covered 5 minutes before serving or refrigerate and when well chilled, slice into 3/4" slices and fry in olive oil or butter. (Or slices may be fried using a microwave browning dish.)

Serves 6

You don't even have to boil the noodles for this one!

MUSHROOM, SPINACH AND GOAT CHEESE LASAGNE

5 ounces soft goat cheese, crumbled
1/2 cup ricotta cheese
7 ounces fresh spinach
8 ounces thinly sliced mushrooms
2 cups prepared spaghetti sauce
2 ounces grated Parmesan cheese
8 ounces grated mozzarella cheese
Salt and freshly ground pepper
3 ounces broad egg noodles, UNCOOKED (not lasagne
     noodles)

1   Combine goat cheese and ricotta, mixing until
     smooth.

2   Combine spinach and mushrooms in a 1 quart micro-
     safe baking dish. Cover with plastic wrap and micro-
     cook on High Power 3-4 minutes, until spinach is just
     barely wilted. Drain spinach and blot gently with
     paper towel.

3   Spread 3/4 cup spaghetti sauce in bottom of the
     baking dish. Top with half the spinach mixture, un-
     folding spinach leaves as necessary. Season lightly
     with salt and pepper.

MUSHROOM, SPINACH AND GOAT CHEESE LASAGNE
continued

4   Cover with 1/2 the uncooked noodles, then a layer of half the goat cheese mixture, half of mozzarella, half of Parmesan and 3/4 cup spaghetti sauce.

5   Top with remaining spinach mixture and season lightly with salt and pepper. Cover with remaining noodles, goat cheese, mozzarella and parmesan. Gently press with a spatula to compress layers. Top with remaining sauce.

6   Cover with plastic wrap and microcook on Medium Power (50%) 24-27 minutes, turning dish occasionally. Let stand covered 5 minutes before serving.

7   Cut into squares and transfer to serving plate using slotted spatula as there may be liquid in bottom of dish.

Serves 4

You can always count on this recipe. No more gummy, boiled over messes. The variations add interesting flavors to your meals.

SUPER SIMPLE PERFECT RICE (PLUS 4 VARIATIONS)

1 cup long grain rice
1 teaspoon salt
1 teaspoon butter or margarine
2 cups water

1   Combine rice, salt, butter and water in a 3 quart microsafe casserole. Cover and microcook on High Power 15-17 minutes.

2   Stir, re-cover and let stand 10-12 minutes and test for doneness. If still crunchy, microcook on High Power 1-2 minutes.

Serves 6-8

For a more flavorful rice, try adding these ingredients before cooking:

HERB BLEND:

1 beef bouillon cube
1/4 teaspoon dried rosemary, crushed
1/4 teaspoon dried thyme, crushed
1/2 teaspoon dried marjoram, crushed
1 teaspoon dry onion flakes

SUPER SIMPLE PERFECT RICE (PLUS 4 VARIATIONS)
continued

CURRIED BLEND:

2 chicken bouillon cubes
1 1/2 teaspoon curry powder
1 teaspoon dry minced onion
1 tablespoon dried mushroom flakes
1/2 teaspoon dried parsley flakes
1/4 teaspoon paprika

ORANGE-RAISIN BLEND:

2 chicken bouillon cubes
2 teaspoons dried orange rind
1/2 cup golden raisins
1/2 cup slivered, toasted almonds

ORANGE-PECAN BLEND:

2 tablespoons fresh orange zest
3/4 cup chopped, toasted pecans (add pecans after rice
    is cooked)

Your microwave performs magic with this marvelous recipe. You'll be amazed at the rich flavor and the ease of preparation.

FAST AND FABULOUS RICE CASSEROLE

1/2 cup butter or margarine, cut in chunks
1 1/3 cups instant rice
1 10 3/4-ounce can onion soup
1/2 cup water
1/3 pound fresh mushrooms, sliced
1/2 teaspoon pepper

1   Place butter, rice, onion soup, water, mushrooms and pepper in a large microsafe casserole. Cover with plastic wrap and microcook on High Power 5 minutes.

2   Stir, re-cover and microcook on Medium Power (50%) 5 minutes.

3   Stir, re-cover and let stand 3 minutes. Serve immediately. Any leftovers may be frozen.

Serves 6-8

This recipe makes a nice addition to a Mexican dinner. It freezes well, so you can prepare it weeks in advance if you wish. Then the leftovers can go back to the freezer.

TEX-MEX RICE

1 cup long grain rice
1/4 cup butter or margarine
1 small onion, chopped
1/2 green pepper, chopped
1 large celery rib, thinly sliced
1 4-ounce can diced green chiles, with liquid
1 8-ounce can tomato sauce
1 14 1/2-ounce can whole tomatoes, with liquid

1   Place the butter and rice in a large microsafe casserole. Microcook on High Power 2 minutes.

2   Add onion, green pepper and celery to rice. Microcook on High Power 7-8 minutes or until rice is slightly brown, stirring once.

3   Add chiles, tomato sauce and tomatoes to the rice mixture. Cover with plastic wrap and microcook on High Power 14-15 minutes, stirring after 10 minutes.

4   Allow to sit covered 5 minutes until all the liquid is absorbed. Serve while hot.

Serves 6-8

This makes a nice starch dish for a buffet dinner or barbecue.

RICE PILAF

2 cups long grain rice
2 10 3/4-ounce cans beef consommé
1 soup can water
2 bunches green onions, sliced, including green parts
1/2 cup butter or margarine

1   Place butter in a microsafe shallow baking dish. Micocook on High Power 1 minute or until just melted. Add uncooked rice and continue to microcook on High Power for 8-10 minutes, stirring often, until rice is dark brown.

2   Remove rice with a slotted spoon and reserve. Add onions to the butter in the casserole, cook and stir in 2 minute intervals, just until onions are limp.

3   Return rice to the casserole. Add consommé and water. Cover with plastic wrap and microcook on High Power for 15 minutes or until no longer crunchy. Stir occasionally while cooking.

Serves 8-10

The cheeses and chiles really dress up this rice casserole.

CHILE CHEESE RICE CASSEROLE

1/2 cup long grain rice
1 cup water
1 cup sour cream
1/4 cup chopped green chiles
1/2 cup sliced ripe olives
1 cup grated Monterey jack cheese
1/2 cup grated cheddar cheese
Paprika, salt and pepper
3 green onions, sliced, including green part

1   Place the rice and water in a large microsafe casserole. Cover with plastic wrap and microcook on High Power 15 minutes. Let stand covered 3 minutes. Fluff with fork.

2   Add sour cream, chiles, sliced olives, jack cheese, salt and pepper to the rice. Stir to combine.

3   Cover with plastic wrap and microcook 4-5 minutes. Top with cheddar cheese, green onion and sprinkling of paprika. Let stand covered 5 minutes.

Serves 6-8

Here is a fast, easy and different way to prepare lasagne. The tomato-sauced green and white pinwheels make a nice presentation.

SPINACH LASAGNE ROLLS

6 lasagne noodles
1 10-ounce package frozen chopped spinach, thawed
1/2 pound lean ground beef
1 medium onion, chopped
1 cup low-fat cottage cheese
1 slightly beaten egg yolk
1 clove garlic, minced
1 teaspoon dried oregano, crushed
1 teaspoon dried basil, crushed
1/4 teaspoon salt
1 15-ounce can herbed tomato sauce
1/4 cup grated Parmesan cheese

1   Cook noodles according to package directions; drain.

2   Thoroughly drain spinach, pressing out excess liquid. Place in a microsafe casserole, cover with plastic wrap and microcook on High Power 5-7 minutes, or until done. Drain.

SPINACH LASAGNE ROLLS   *continued*

3   Crumble beef into a microsafe pie plate. Stir in onion.
Microcook on High Power 3-5 minutes or until beef is
done, stirring once to break up meat. Drain off fat.
Or use colander method (see 101 Quick Tricks,
Ground Beef - cooking).

4   Combine cottage cheese, egg yolk, garlic, oregano,
basil and salt. Stir cottage cheese mixture and meat
mixture into spinach.

5   Spread some of the mixture on each lasagne noodle.
Roll up jellyroll fashion, starting with short edge. Place
seam side down in a 10 x 6 x 2 inch microsafe casserole. Pour tomato sauce over rolls and microcook on
High Power 10-12 minutes or until heated through.

6   Sprinkle cheese on each roll and serve.

Serves 6

No added butter or oil in this one! I developed this recipe for a cooking class I gave at a fitness center. Class members thought it was quite wonderful and especially liked the crunchiness of the vegetables and nuts.

PINE NUT VEGETABLE PILAF

1 cup long grain rice
2 cups water
1/2 teaspoon salt
1/4 teaspoon ground white pepper
2 stalks celery, thinly sliced
I large carrot, thinly sliced
2 tablespoons snipped fresh chives
1/2 cup toasted pine nuts (toast on plate in Microwave
     oven-High Power 3-4 minutes, stirring every 2 minutes)
1/2 teaspoon lemon zest
1/2 teaspoon dried thyme
2 tablespoons minced fresh parsley

1   Combine rice, water, salt and pepper in a large microsafe casserole. Cover with plastic wrap and microcook on High Power 17 minutes. Fluff with a fork, re-cover and let stand while preparing vegetables.

2   Combine sliced celery and sliced carrot in a microsafe dish, cover with plastic wrap and microcook on High Power 2-3 minutes or until crisp tender.

3   Toss vegetables with the warm rice. Add chives, toasted pine nuts, lemon zest, thyme and parsley to the rice mixture and toss again to mix. Cover with plastic wrap and microcook on High Power 3-4 minutes or until heated through. Serve warm.

Serves 6-8 (Leftovers may be frozen and small portions easily reheated in the microwave).

10

SAUCES

Rum Sauce
Cranberry Chutney
Cranberry Relish
Cold Cucumber Sauce
German Mustard
Easy White Sauce
Hollandaise Sauce
Foolproof Bernaise Sauce
Bengal Chutney
White Clam Sauce for Pasta
Walnut Sauce for Pasta
Pesto Sauce for Pasta
Superb Alfredo Sauce for Pasta
Marvelous Microwave Marmalade

Another holiday sauce to have on hand. Takes only minutes to make and reheats beautifully.

RUM SAUCE

1/2 cup sugar
2 tablespoons cornstarch
1 teaspoon salt
1 1/2 cup milk
1/4 cup butter or margarine
1/8 teaspoon nutmeg
1/2 cup rum

1   Combine sugar, cornstarch and salt in a large micro-safe bowl.   Gradually stir in milk.

2   Add butter to mixture, microwave on High Power 6 minutes, or until sauce is thickened and clear, stirring every 2 minutes. If more cooking is necessary, cook on High Power in 30 second intervals, until desired temperature and consistency are reached.

3   Stir in nutmeg and rum. Serve warm over apple pie, dessert crèpes, plum pudding etc.

Makes 2 cups (Refrigerated sauce keeps well for several weeks and is easily reheated in the microwave.)

This fabulous chutney does double duty! You might serve it with your holiday turkey OR with crackers and cream cheese at your holiday party. Makes a lovely gift when spooned into a decorative jar, topped with a circle of festive fabric and tied with colorful yarn.

CRANBERRY CHUTNEY

1/4 cup water
1/4 cup cider vinegar
1/2 cup brown sugar
1/2 cup chopped onion
1/2 cup raisins
1/2 cup chopped dates
1 clove garlic, minced
1 teaspoon cinnamon
1/4 teaspoon ground cloves
1/2 teaspoon salt
1/8 teaspoon cayenne pepper
3 tablespoons diced crystalized ginger
2 cups raw cranberries

1   Place water, cider vinegar, brown sugar, chopped onion, raisins, dates, garlic, cinnamon, cloves, salt, cayenne pepper and ginger in a large microsafe bowl. Microcook on High Power for 8 minutes. Add cranberries and microcook on High Power 5 minutes.

2   Store in refrigerator or freeze.

3   Serve hot or cold.

Makes 3 cups

Another easy but special holiday necessity. The addition of apple, orange and walnuts really sparks this lovely relish.

CRANBERRY RELISH

1 pound fresh cranberries
1 cup sugar
1 cup water
1 cup currant jelly
1/2 cup raisins or currants
1/2 cup walnuts or pecans, coarsely broken
1 orange, including peel, grated in food processor
1 red unpeeled apple, chopped

1   Place cranberries, sugar, water and currant jelly in a large microsafe bowl. Microcook on High Power 10-12 minutes or until boiling and cranberries "mush" when stirred.

2   Stir in raisins, nuts, grated orange and chopped apple. Cool and refrigerate.

Makes 1 1/2 quarts

Sauce cold poached salmon with this creamy mixture for a lovely entrée on a warm summer evening.

COLD CUCUMBER SAUCE

1 large cucumber, peeled, seeded and grated
1/2 cup mayonnaise
1/2 cup sour cream
2 teaspoons Dijon mustard
2 teaspoons lemon juice
1/4 teaspoon salt
1/8 teaspoon pepper
1/4 cup snipped fresh dill
2 tablespoons finely chopped fresh chives.

1   Combine all ingredients and mix well. Refrigerate until serving time.

2   This sauce can be served with cold poached salmon for an outstanding entrée or elegant summer lunch. (see index for Cold Poached Salmon recipe).

Makes 1 cup

Make up some of this yummy mustard and put into small jars to give as gifts. (Don't forget to save some for yourself).

GERMAN MUSTARD

1 cup dry mustard
1 cup cider vinegar
2 eggs
3/4 cup sugar

1   Combine mustard and cider vinegar in microsafe bowl. Mix and let stand covered at room temperature for 24 hours.

2   Beat eggs with sugar and stir into mustard mixture. Microcook on Medium Power (50%) 3 minutes. Stir and check the consistency. Continue to cook and stir in 30 second intervals, until thick.

Makes 1 1/2 cups

You will never use your cooktop white sauce once you've tried this easy, easy method.

EASY WHITE SAUCE

3 tablespoons butter or margarine
3 tablespoons flour
1/4 teaspoon salt
1/8 teaspoon pepper
1 cup milk

1   Place butter in medium sized microsafe bowl or 1
     quart glass measure. Microcook on High Power 30
     seconds, or until melted.

2   Stir in flour, salt and pepper. Microcook on High
     Power 4 seconds.

3   Stir until smooth, whisk in milk and microcook on High
     2 minutes.

4   Stir. Microcook on High Power in 30 second intervals,
     until desired consistency is achieved. If too thick, thin
     with milk.

Makes 1 cup

You'll sauce lots of things with this wonderful foolproof Hollandaise. Just remember to cook it on Medium Power (50%).

HOLLANDAISE SAUCE

1/2 cup butter, cut into pieces
2 tablespoons lemon juice
1/2 teaspoon Dijon mustard
2 drops red pepper sauce
2 egg yolks

1 Place butter pieces in a microsafe bowl. Microcook on High Power 1 minute. Pour into processor work bowl or blender.

2 Add lemon juice, mustard and hot sauce to processor bowl. Insert steel knife, process mixture until blended.

3 Add egg yolks, one at a time, through feed tube, processing 30 seconds after each addition.

4 Pour sauce into a microsafe bowl and microcook on Medium Power (50%) until thick, about 1 1/2 minutes, stirring after 1 minute. Do not use a higher power to cook the sauce as it will curdle and separate.

Makes 3/4 cup (This sauce refrigerates well for several days and reheats beautifully on Medium Power or lower. Whole eggs may be used instead of just the yolks. This will make a fluffier hollandaise.)

A lovely sauce for broiled beef. Takes minutes to make instead of the usual tedious cooktop method.

FOOLPROOF BERNAISE SAUCE

Make Easy White Sauce (see index)
1 small onion, chopped
1 1/2 teaspoons dried tarragon
1/4 cup white wine vinegar
2 tablespoons chopped parsley
3 beaten egg yolks
3 tablespoons butter or margarine
5 teaspoons lemon juice

1   Combine onion, tarragon, vinegar and parsley in microsafe bowl. Microcook on High Power 3 minutes or until mixture is slightly reduced.

2   To white sauce add egg yolks, butter and lemon juice. Stir well and add onion-tarragon mixture. Microcook on High Power 1-2 minutes or until thickened and heated through.

Makes 1 1/4 cups

This spicy chutney is a perfect addition to any curry dinner.

BENGAL CHUTNEY

3 cloves garlic, minced
1 medium onion, chopped
3 pounds tart apples, peeled, cored and sliced
1 small lemon, sliced
3 cups brown sugar, packed
2 cups cider vinegar
1 cup golden raisins
1 tablespoon mustard seed
2 teaspoons ground ginger
1/2 teaspoon salt
1/4 teaspoon crushed red pepper flakes

1   Place all ingredients in a large microsafe bowl.
     Microcook on High Power 6-8 minutes or until boiling.
     Cover with plastic wrap and microcook on Medium
     Power (50%) until sauce is thickened and apples are
     tender.

2   Cool and store covered in refrigerator up to three
     months.

Makes 5-6 cups

This garlicky clam sauce is a nice change from the usual tomato and meat sauce.

WHITE CLAM SAUCE FOR PASTA

1/2 cup butter or margarine
1/4 cup olive oil
2 cloves garlic, minced
2 7-ounce cans chopped clams, undrained
1 teaspoon dried basil
1 teaspoon dried oregano
1/4 teaspoon crushed red pepper
1 1/2 cups chopped fresh parsley

1   Place butter in microsafe bowl. Microcook on High Power 1 minute or until melted.

2   Add olive oil, juice from clams, basil, oregano, red pepper, minced garlic and chopped parsley. Microcook on High Power 3-4 minutes, until hot.

3   Add drained clams to butter-herb mixture and microcook on Medium Power (50%) 3-4 minutes, until clams are just heated through. (Don't overcook as the clams will toughen).

4   Toss with 1 pound cooked pasta and serve immediately.

Makes 1 1/2 cups

*The editors of Bon Appétit magazine liked my Walnut
Sauce so much they printed it in the magazine and in a
recent cookbook!*

WALNUT SAUCE FOR PASTA

2 cups milk
6 tablespoons butter or margarine
1/4 cup grated Swiss cheese
1/4 cup freshly grated Parmesan cheese
1/4 cup flour
1 teaspoon salt
1/4 teaspoon white pepper
2 tablespoons coarsely chopped walnuts
Freshly grated nutmeg

1   Place milk in large microsafe bowl. Microcook on
     High Power for 2 minutes.

2   Stir in butter, cheeses, flour, salt and pepper. Micro-
     cook on High Power, stirring frequently, until slightly
     thickened, 4-5 minutes.

3   Add walnuts and nutmeg and mix well.

4   Add sauce to freshly cooked pasta (1 pound) and
     toss. Serve immediately. Pass additional Parmesan
     cheese and nutmeg with grater.

Makes 2 cups sauce

Brown the pine nuts and make this wonderful pasta sauce for an easy and economical dinner for family or friends.

PESTO SAUCE FOR PASTA

2 cups lightly packed fresh basil leaves, washed and
      patted dry
1 cup grated Parmesan cheese
1/2 cup olive oil
2 cloves garlic, minced
1/2 cup pine nuts
1/4 cup butter or margarine
8 ounces fresh cooked pasta

1   Place pine nuts on microsafe plate. Microcook on High Power 3-5 minutes, until light brown, stirring occasionally. Set nuts aside.

2   Place basil, cheese and oil in processor; process using steel blade. Add garlic and pine nuts to mixture, pulse just to combine.

3   Place butter in a microsafe bowl and microcook on High Power 30 seconds. Add 6 tablespoons previously made pesto sauce and grated Parmesan cheese, mix well. Microcook on High Power 1 minute, to heat slightly. Pour sauce over hot cooked, drained fettuccine or other pasta. Toss gently. Serve additonal cheese.

Makes 1 cup (If you wish to keep the pesto for later use, add a thin layer of olive oil on top to keep the pesto from darkening. Refrigerate for 1 week or freeze.)

Treat your family to this wonderful yet easy classic Alfredo Sauce.

SUPERB ALFREDO SAUCE FOR PASTA

1/2 cup butter or margarine
2 cups sour cream
1 tablespoon flour
3/4 cup Parmesan cheese
1/4 cup dry vermouth
2 tablespoons lemon juice
1/2 teaspoon marjoram
1/2 teaspoon oregano
1/2 teaspoon dried basil
Salt and pepper

1   Place butter in microsafe bowl or casserole. Micro-cook on High Power 1 minute or until melted.

2   Stir in sour cream, flour, Parmesan cheese, dry vermouth, lemon juice, marjoram, oregano, basil, salt and pepper to taste. Microcook on Medium Power (50%) 3-5 minutes, stirring often.

3   Toss with 1 pound cooked fettucini. Serve immediately.

Makes 2 cups

This recipe of mine was featured in an issue of Bon Appétit and in a cookbook, complete with a colored photo. You'll never buy marmalade again once you've tried this marvelous recipe.

MARVELOUS MICROWAVE MARMALADE

1 navel orange, unpeeled
Sugar
Light corn syrup

1   Shred entire orange in processor, using grating blade. Measure grated orange and transfer to 1 quart microsafe bowl.

2   Measure enough sugar to equal amount of orange. Add to bowl.

3   Add 1 tablespoon light corn syrup for every cup of orange-sugar mixture. (corn syrup helps prevent crystalizing)

4   Microcook, stirring occasionally, on Medium Power (50%) 6 minutes or until slightly thickened. Do not overcook.

5   Store covered in refrigerator until ready to use.

6   To make a larger batch combine equal amounts of grated orange and sugar plus 1 tablespoon light corn syrup per cup of orange-sugar mixture. Increase cooking time. You may also add brandy or drained crushed pineapple for a little different flavor.

Makes 2/3 cup (Little jars of this marmalade along with a copy of the recipe make nice gifts for family friends and neighbors.)

11

CAKES, COOKIES AND CANDY

Cheese Cake Elegante
Carrot Cake
Banana Pecan Rum Cake
White Chocolate Crisps
Crunchy Chocolate Cookies
Chocolate Shortbread Cookies
Peanut Butter Cookies
Lemon Wedges
Butterscotch Crispies
Toffee Bars
Peanut Butter Bars
Crème de Menthe Bars
Easy Almond Roca
Walnut Bark
Perfect Peanut Brittle

Another classic recipe, simplified by using the microwave.

CHEESE CAKE ELEGANTE

1/3 cup butter
30 graham cracker squares, crushed
1/4 cup powdered sugar
1 teaspoon allspice
2 8-ounce packages cream cheese
2 eggs, beaten
2/3 cups sugar
2 teaspoons vanilla
1 1/2 cups sour cream
4 tablespoons sugar
2 teaspoons vanilla

1   Place butter in a 10 inch microsafe pie plate. Micro-
     cook on High Power 30 seconds. Add graham
     cracker crumbs, powdered sugar and allspice. Pat
     firmly into bottom and sides of the pie plate. Micro-
     cook on High Power 2 minutes 30 seconds. Cool.

2   Place cream cheese bars in a microsafe bowl and
     soften by microcooking on Medium Power (50%) 2-3
     minutes. Stir until soft and creamy. Add eggs, sugar
     and vanilla. Beat until thoroughly creamed and
     smooth. Microcook on High Power 4 minutes, stirring
     once during cooking.

3   Pour into crust and microcook on High Power 1-2
     minutes. Cool 5 minutes.

4   Combine sour cream, sugar and remaining 2 tea-
     spoons vanilla in a microsafe bowl. Microcook on
     High Power 1-2 minutes, stirring once. Cool, spread
     over cheesecake and refrigerate until firm.

Serves 12

The flavor and texture of this classic favorite is enhanced by cooking in the microwave. Try it and see!

CARROT CAKE

3 eggs
1 1/2 cups sugar
1 cup oil
1 teaspoon vanilla
1 1/2 cups flour
3/4 teaspoon salt
1 1/4 teaspoons baking soda
2 1/2 teaspoons cinnamon
1 1/4 teaspoons ground cloves
2 1/2 cups grated carrots (4-5 medium-size carrots)
3/4 cup coarsely chopped walnuts

1   In mixer bowl or processor, combine eggs, sugar, oil and vanilla. Add flour, salt, baking soda, cinnamon and cloves. Fold in carrots and nuts.

2   Pour into a 12 cup microsafe greased bundt pan. Place in microwave oven on a plastic rack or inverted microsafe bowl. Microcook on High Power 12-14 minutes, rotating 1/4 turn twice during cooking. Cake is done when it pulls away from side of pan.

3   Let rest 10 minutes, loosen sides and center; invert on serving plate. Frost with Cream Cheese Frosting.

CARROT CAKE

continued

Frosting:

4 ounces cream cheese
3 tablespoons butter or margarine
2 cups powdered sugar
1 teaspoon vanilla

1   Place cream cheese and butter in a small microsafe
     bowl. Microcook on High Power 1 minute. Blend in
     powdered sugar and vanilla. Beat until light and
     fluffy.

2   Microcook on High Power 30 seconds to 1 minute, or
     until slightly runny. Drizzle over cake.

Frosting: 1 1/2 cups
Cake serves 10

A cake for company, made easily with a few packages, the microwave, bananas, pecans and rum.

BANANA PECAN RUM CAKE

1 tablespoon sugar
1 tablespoon cinnamon
1 package yellow cake mix
1 3-3/4-ounce package vanilla pudding
4 eggs
1/2 cup vegetable oil
1/2 cup buttermilk
1 1/2 teaspoons vanilla
1 cup mashed bananas
3/4 cup chopped pecans

Glaze:
1/2 cup butter or margarine
1 cup sugar
1/4 cup rum

1   Sprinkle sugar and cinnamon into a lightly oiled microsafe bundt pan.

2   Combine cake mix, vanilla pudding, eggs, vegetable oil, buttermilk, bananas and pecans.

BANANA PECAN RUM CAKE   *continued*

3   Pour batter into prepared bundt pan and cover
     loosely with waxed paper. Place in microwave oven
     on a rack or an inverted microsafe dish. Microcook
     on Medium Power (50%) 9-10 minutes or until it begins
     to pull away from sides of pan.

4   While cake is cooling slightly, combine the glaze
     ingredients. Place butter in a medium size microsafe
     bowl. Microcook on High Power 1 minute. Add sugar
     and rum; microcook on High Power 2 minutes 30
     seconds.

5   Pour over the warm cake and let sit 1/2 hour.

Serves 8-10

The pretzels in this easy, easy recipe add a unique flavor. The haystack type mounds make an interesting contrast to the usual plate of holiday cookies.

WHITE CHOCOLATE CRISPS

1 pound white chocolate, broken into small pieces
2 cups stick pretzels, broken in half
2 cups red skinned salted Spanish peanuts

1   Place white chocolate pieces in a large microsafe bowl. Microcook on High Power 2 minutes 30 seconds, stirring once while cooking. Don't be fooled; chocolate keeps its shape even though melted. If further cooking is required, microcook on High Power in 30 second intervals until smooth when stirred. Do not overcook.

2   Add broken pretzels and Spanish peanuts; mix until well coated. Drop by spoonfuls onto waxed paper.

3   Cookies will harden in a few hours. To speed hardening, refrigerate.

Makes 48

Another fast and easy drop cookie. Nice to have on hand during the holidays to serve to unexpected guests with a cup of coffee or tea.

CRUNCHY CHOCOLATE COOKIES

2 6-ounce packages chocolate chips
1 14-ounce can sweetened condensed milk
    (not evaporated)
1 teaspoon vanilla
1 cup grapenuts cereal

1   Place chocolate chips in a microsafe bowl. Micro-cook on High Power 2 minutes-stir. Continue to cook and stir in 30 second intervals until melted and smooth. Do not overcook.

2   Add sweetened condensed milk and vanilla. Stir until smooth. Stir in grapenuts and drop in small mounds on a sheet of waxed paper. Let sit at room temperature to solidify or refrigerate to harden more quickly. These can be frozen for later use.

Makes 36

Yes, you really can bake cookies in the microwave. Just try these and see. Cooking time 2 minutes per batch? WOW!

CHOCOLATE SHORTBREAD COOKIES

2 ounces semi-sweet chocolate, broken into pieces
2/3 cup pecans, chopped
2 2/3 cups flour
3/4 cup powdered sugar
1 cup cold butter
1 tablespoon vanilla
Cocoa or powdered sugar

1   Grate chocolate fine. Mix together the flour, pow-dered sugar, butter and vanilla.

2   Add pecans and grated chocolate and mix until smooth. Chocolate pieces will be visible in dough.

3   Roll into balls. Place 12 balls in a circle on a waxed paper lined microsafe tray. Flatten cookies with bottom of a drinking glass. Microcook, uncovered, on High Power, 2 - 2 1/2 minutes, rotating dish 1/4 turn after 1 minute. Cookies should be firm and slightly crisp.

4   Let stand 5 minutes, remove and cool on wire rack. Cookies will become crisper as they cool.

5   Repeat with remaining dough. Sprinkle cookies with cocoa or powdered sugar. Store at room tempera-ture in airtight container.

Makes 36

These are even better than the ones Mother used to make!

PEANUT BUTTER COOKIES

1/2 cup vegetable shortening
1/2 cup sugar
1/2 cup brown sugar
1/2 cup peanut butter
1 beaten egg
1 1/2 cups flour
1/4 teaspoon baking soda
1/4 teaspoon salt
1 teaspoon vanilla

1   Cream shortening and sugars, add peanut butter
    and egg and mix well.

2   Blend in flour, soda, salt and vanilla. Shape into 36
    balls.

3   Arrange 12 balls on a waxed paper lined microsafe
    tray, spacing cookies in a circle 2 inches apart.
    Flatten with a fork dipped in flour.

4   Microcook on High Power, 1 minute 30 seconds,
    rotate tray and microcook 1 more minute.

5   Leaving cookies on the waxed paper, carefully slide
    paper off tray. Let cookies cool on waxed paper.

6   Cook remaining cookies in same manner. Because
    of the high sugar and shortening content of these
    cookies, they can burn easily from the inside out, not
    on the bottom. Do not overcook.

Makes 36

These will disappear quickly, but you can easily make more, thanks to your microwave oven. Notice you use only one cooking dish in this recipe.

LEMON WEDGES

1/2 cup butter
1 cup flour
1/4 teaspoon salt
1/4 cup powdered sugar
2 eggs, beaten
1 cup sugar
3 tablespoon lemon juice
2 tablespoons flour
1/2 teaspoon baking powder
Sifted powdered sugar

1   Place butter in a microsafe 9-inch pie plate. Micro-cook on High 45-60 seconds. Stir in flour, salt and powdered sugar. Press evenly in pie plate. Micro-cook on Medium High Power (70%) 3-4 minutes, rotating halfway through cooking. Cook until bubbly on top.

2   Combine egg, sugar, lemon juice, flour and baking powder. Pour over previously prepared crust. Micro-cook on Medium High Power (70%) 5-7 minutes or until lemon mixture becomes fairly firm.

3   Sprinkle with sifted powdered sugar. Cool and cut into small wedges.

Makes 12-16 wedges

Little ones love to make these yummy cookies. The micro-wave makes it safe and easy.

BUTTERSCOTCH CRISPIES

1 12-ounce package butterscotch chips
3 tablespoons peanut butter
5 cups cornflakes

1   Place butterscotch chips and peanut butter in a 3 quart microsafe bowl, microcook on High Power 2 minutes, stir. Mixture should be smooth and creamy. If tiny morsels of chips remain, microcook 30 seconds and stir well.

2   Combine the peanut butter mixture with cornflakes until flakes are well coated. Drop in small mounds on a sheet of waxed paper. Let stand at room tempera-ture to solidify. Store in refrigerator or an air tight container.

Makes 36

This is a delicious toffee bar cookie. Your friends will never know how simple they are to make.

TOFFEE BARS

15 graham cracker squares
1 cup brown sugar
1 cup butter or margarine
3/4 cup chopped walnuts
3/4 pound milk chocolate bars without nuts

1   (Be certain that your microwave oven can accommodate a 9 x 15 inch microsafe baking dish). Line bottom of an 9 x 15 inch baking dish with graham cracker squares. They should fit perfectly.

2   Combine butter and sugar in a large microsafe bowl. Cook on High 2 1/2 - 3 minutes, stirring occasionally. When mixture boils, microcook on High Power 2 more minutes.

3   Pour the hot butter-sugar mixture over graham crackers, sprinkle chopped walnuts evenly over top and lay a piece of waxed paper loosely over the top of the dish. Microcook on High Power 4 minutes.

4   Lay chocolate bars evenly over top, return dish to microwave and microcook 1 minute. Remove from oven and spread chocolate evenly over top. (Remember chocolate will retain its shape even though melted. Don't be fooled.)

5   Refrigerate until firm. For ease in cutting, let warm to room temperature before cutting into bars.

Makes 48 bars

This candy type bar has been well received by my students. If you like peanut butter cups you'll love these. They freeze beautifully!

PEANUT BUTTER BARS

1 cup butter
1 cup peanut butter
30 graham cracker squares
2 cups powdered sugar
1 6-ounce package chocolate chips
2 tablespoons solid shortening

1   Place butter and peanut butter in a microsafe bowl. Microcook on High Power for 2 1/2 - 3 minutes.

2   Crush graham cracker squares in processor or put crackers between 2 sheets of waxed paper and crush with rolling pin. Combine with powdered sugar. Add peanut butter mixture. Stir until combined and pat into a 3 quart rectangular baking dish.

3   Combine chocolate chips and solid shortening in a microsafe bowl and microcook on High Power for 2 1/2 - 3 minutes. Be sure to stir the chips. They will retain their shape, even though melted.

4   Spread the chocolate mixture evenly over the peanut butter layer and refrigerate.

5   Warm to room temperature, cut into small squares and serve as a candy. These freeze well.

Makes 40 squares

An elegant bar, made quickly and easily with the aid of the microwave.

CRÈME DE MENTHE BARS

<u>Crust</u>:
1/3 cup butter or margarine
1/3 cup cocoa
22 graham cracker squares, crushed
1 egg
1 teaspoon vanilla
1/2 cup chopped walnuts

<u>Filling</u>:
1/3 cup butter or margarine
1/4 cup green crème de menthe
2 1/2 cups powdered sugar

<u>Topping</u>:
1 6-ounce package chocolate chips
2 tablespoons butter or margarine

1   Place butter in a 2 quart rectangular microsafe
     baking dish. Microcook on High Power 1 minute.

CRÈME DE MENTHE BARS   *continued*

2   Add cocoa, graham cracker crumbs, egg, vanilla and chopped walnuts. Mix well and press evenly over bottom of dish Microcook on Medium Power (50%) 2-3 minutes. Let cool.

3   For filling, place butter in microsafe bowl and micro-cook on High Power 1 minute. Add crème de menthe and sugar. Mix well and spread over chocolate layer and chill.

4   Make topping by combining butter and chocolate chips in a microsafe bowl and cooking on Medium-High Power (70%) 1-2 minutes. Stir and spread evenly over the green crème de menthe layer.

5   Chill and cut into small squares. You might serve these candies in small petits fours papers.

Makes 36 bars

A neighbor of mine can hardly wait to get this recipe as she craves the old-fashioned Heath Bars. It's important to cook the sugar syrup to the soft crack stage for perfect candy.

EASY ALMOND ROCA

1/2 cup butter or margarine
1 1/2 cups sugar
3 tablespoons water
1 tablespoon light corn syrup
4 1-1/5 ounce milk chocolate candy bars
1/2 cup finely chopped almonds

1   Place butter in a large microsafe bowl. Microcook on High Power 1-2 minutes or until melted. Stir in sugar, water and corn syrup. Microcook on High Power 8-9 minutes or to soft crack stage, (i.e. a small drop of syrup dropped into cold water separates into threads that are hard but not brittle.)

2   Pour onto well greased waxed paper; let stand 1 minute.

3   Break chocolate bars into small pieces and sprinkle over candy. As chocolate melts, spread evenly.

4   Gently press nuts into chocolate.

5   Chill until chocolate is set. Break into small pieces. Store at room temperature in an airtight container.

Makes 1 1/4 pounds

Don't be surprised if you get lots of raves over this candy. Don't tell them how fast and simple it is.

WALNUT BARK

1 cup walnuts, coarsely chopped
1 teaspoon butter
1 pound white chocolate, broken into pieces

1   Combine walnuts and butter on a microsafe plate. Microcook on High Power 4-5 minutes, stirring once or twice, cooking until walnuts are toasted.

2   Line baking sheet with waxed paper and set aside. Place chocolate in a microsafe bowl and microcook on High Power 1 1/2 - 2 minutes. Do not overcook or chocolate will become grainy. (If you should over-cook the chocolate, add 1 tablespoon butter and reheat briefly, stir well.)

3   Stir walnuts into chocolate, blend well and spread mixture onto previously prepared baking sheet. Refrigerate until set. Break into pieces. Store in refrigerator. (Almonds can be substituted for the walnuts).

Makes 1 1/2 pounds

This candy couldn't be better! Just be certain to cook to the hard crack stage or you will have chewy peanut brittle, instead of hard crisp peanut brittle.

PERFECT PEANUT BRITTLE

1 cup sugar
1/2 cup dark corn syrup
2 cups dry roasted unsalted peanuts
1 teaspoon butter
1 teaspoon vanilla
1 teaspoon baking soda

1   Grease a metal baking sheet and place it near microwave for easy access later.

2   Combine sugar and corn syrup in a 2 or 3 quart microsafe bowl. Microcook on High Power 3 minutes.

3   Stir in peanuts, butter and vanilla. Microcook on High Power 6 minutes or until small amount of mixture separates into hard and brittle threads when dropped into very cold water (hard crack stage.) This is one time you don't want to undercook, as you'll get chewy instead of brittle candy.

4   Quickly blend in baking soda, stirring until mixture is light and foamy. Pour immediately onto previously prepared baking sheet, spreading toward edges.

5   Let cool completely. Break into pieces. Store in an airtight container or zip-lock bag at room temperature.

Makes 1 pound

12

PIES AND OTHER DESSERTS

Mud Pie
Grasshopper Pie
French Silk Pie
Frozen Lemon Pie
Marshmallow Pie
Individual Fruit Tarts in Nut Crumb Crusts
Orange Chocolate Mousse
Pears with Flaming Raspberry Sauce
Bananas Foster
Butter Pecan Ice Cream
Frozen Strawberry Dessert
Pots De Crème

Our two daughters used to think this was pure heaven! (I think they still crave it!) The ingredients are few and simple and they go together quickly thanks to the microwave.

MUD PIE

30 chocolate cream-filled sandwich type cookies, crushed
    into crumbs
1/4 cup butter or margarine
1 quart coffee ice cream
Fudge ice cream topping (not chocolate syrup)

1   Place butter in a 9-inch microsafe pie plate. Micro-cook on High Power 30 seconds. Add crumbs to butter, mix well and pat into bottom and sides of pie plate.

2   Place the carton of coffee ice cream in the micro-wave and microcook on Defrost or Low Power (10%) 1-2 minutes or until soft enough to spoon evenly into cookie crust shell. Place in freezer.

3   When well frozen, remove pie from freezer. Spoon 1 cup Fudge topping into a microsafe bowl and micro-cook on High Power 45-60 seconds. Spread softened fudge topping over frozen pie. Return pie to freezer until serving time.

4   May be topped with whipped cream and grated chocolate if you really want to be decadent!

Serves 8

This cool green pie with its contrasting chocolate crust and chocolate leaves or curls makes a refreshing statement after a meal.

GRASSHOPPER PIE

16 chocolate cream-filled sandwich type cookies, crushed
    into crumbs
2 tablespoons butter or margarine
24 large marshmallows
1/2 cup milk
1/4 cup white crème de cocoa
1/4 cup green crème de menthe
1 cup whipping cream, whipped
Green food coloring
Chocolate leaves (see index) or chocolate curls
    (see index)

1   Place butter in a microsafe 9-inch pie plate. Micro-
     cook on High Power 30 seconds. Combine the
     crushed cookies with melted butter and mix well. Pat
     firmly into bottom and sides of pie plate.

2   Combine marshmallows and milk in a large microsafe
     bowl. Microcook on High Power 2 minutes. Stir well
     and continue cooking on High Power in 1 minute
     intervals until marshmallows are melted and mixture is
     smooth and creamy, 4-6 minutes. Cool the mixture.

3   Add crème de cocoa and crème de menthe to the
     cooled marshmallow mixture.

4   Gently fold in whipped cream and tint to shade
     desired with green food coloring.

5   Mound into previously prepared crust and top with
     semi-sweet chocolate leaves or chocolate curls.
     Cover and refrigerate.

Serves 6-8

This is an easy yet elegant pie to serve at your next dinner party. The chocolate leaves help to make this a picture-perfect presentation.

FRENCH SILK PIE

22 graham cracker squares, crushed into crumbs
3 tablespoons sugar
6 tablespoons butter
3 ounces unsweetened chocolate
3 tablespoons butter
1/2 cup sugar
1/4 cup brown sugar
1 teaspoon vanilla
3 eggs
1/2 pint cream, whipped
Chocolate leaves (see index for recipe)

1   Place butter in a 10-inch microsafe pie plate. Micro-cook on High Power 30 seconds or until melted. Add cracker crumbs and sugar.

2   Blend well and press mixture on bottom and sides of pie plate. Microcook on High Power 1 1/2 minutes, rotating plate after 1 minute. Cool.

3   Place chocolate in a large, microsafe bowl. Micro-cook on High Power 2-3 minutes or until chocolate is melted and smooth when stirred with a spoon. Add butter and sugars and mix well with electric mixer until light and fluffy. Add vanilla.

4   Add eggs one at a time blending well after each addition. Spoon mixture into prepared crust and refrigerate until filling is set, 4-6 hours or overnight.

5   To serve, slice into wedges and place on serving plates. Top each serving with a dollop of whipped cream and arrange chocolate leaves on top.

Serves 8

My mother used to make this for company and my sister and I would fight over the left-overs. It's so easy to make, thanks to the microwave, that you can treat your family often. Don't make it just for company.

FROZEN LEMON PIE

3 egg yolks
1/4 cup lemon juice
lemon zest (outer rind of lemon finely grated) from 1/2
     lemon
1/2 cup sugar
1/4 teaspoon salt
2 tablespoons sugar
3 egg whites
1 cup whipping cream, whipped
22 graham cracker squares, crushed into crumbs

1   Combine egg yolks, lemon juice, lemon zest, sugar and salt in a microsafe bowl. Microcook on High Power in 1 minute intervals, stirring after each cooking period. Cook until thick and smooth, about 4-6 minutes. Let custard cool.

2   Whip egg whites until stiff. Gently fold whipped egg whites into the cooled custard mixture.

3   Carefully fold whipped cream into the custard mixture.

4   Sprinkle 1/2 the graham cracker crumbs into bottom of a 10 inch pie plate. Spoon cream-custard mixture over crumbs. Spoon remaining crumbs on top, pressing into whipped mixture slightly, and freeze. Garnish individual portions with lemon slices and lemon or mint leaves if you wish.

Serves 8-10

Aunt Helen used to make this pie for family gatherings and my cousins and I loved it. Now this generation can make it too, but so much faster using a microwave.

MARSHMALLOW PIE

22 graham cracker squares, crushed into crumbs
1/4 cup sugar
1/3 cup butter or margarine
24 large marshmallows
1/2 cup milk
1 cup whipping cream, whipped
1/2 cup semi-sweet chocolate chips
1/2 cup walnuts, coarsely chopped

1   Place the butter in a 9 inch microsafe pie plate. Microcook on High Power 45 seconds. Combine graham cracker crumbs and sugar with butter and press firmly into sides and bottom of pie plate. Microcook crust on High Power 1 1/2-2 minutes or until set. Let cool.

2   Combine marshmallows and milk in a large microsafe bowl. Microcook on High Power 2 minutes. Stir well and continue cooking in 1 minute intervals until marshmallows are melted and mixture is smooth and creamy. Cool the mixture slightly and fold in whipped cream.

3   Carefully fold in chocolate chips and walnuts. Mound into prepared graham cracker crust and refrigerate several hours or overnight.

Serves 6-8

The perfect dessert to serve on a warm summer evening.

INDIVIDUAL FRUIT TARTS IN NUT CRUMB CRUSTS

<u>Toasted Nut Crumb Crust</u>:

1/2 cup chopped pecans or walnuts
6 tablespoons butter or margarine
3 tablespoons sugar
15 graham crackers (2 1/2 inches square), crushed

1   Place chopped nuts and butter in a microsafe bowl and microcook on High Power 3-5 minutes or until toasted, stirring occasionally .

2   Combine nuts, sugar and cracker crumbs and press into bottoms of six 4-inch metal tartlet pans. Do not bake. Refrigerate until ready to assemble tarts.

<u>Pastry Cream</u>:

1/2 cup sugar
1/3 cup flour
3 egg yolks
1 cup whipping cream
2 tablespoons almond or orange flavored liqueur
1/2 teaspoon vanilla

<u>Fruit Layer</u>:

Assorted fresh fruit: peaches, pineapple, kiwi, strawberries,
        bananas, raspberries, melon, etc. or frozen fruit,
        thawed and drained
3/4 cup peach or apricot preserves

INDIVIDUAL FRUIT TARTS IN NUT CRUMB CRUSTS

continued

1   Combine sugar and flour, add egg yolks and beat until thick and lemon colored.

2   Place cream in a microsafe bowl and microcook on High Power 1-3 minutes, just until boiling. Very slowly pour the hot cream into the egg mixture beating continuously. Microcook on Medium High Power (70%) until thickened, 5-7 minutes, stirring every 2 minutes.

3   Stir in liqueur and vanilla. Cool to room temperature. Refrigerate.

4   To assemble tarts, spoon Pastry Cream into Tart crusts and arrange fruit decoratively over tops. Microcook preserves on High Power 1 minute or until melted. Brush preserves over fruit and refrigerate. Remove tarts from pans and serve within 2 hours or tarts may become soggy.

Serves 6

A gelatin based mousse made quickly and effortlessly in the microwave.

ORANGE CHOCOLATE MOUSSE

2 eggs
3 egg yolks
1/2 cup sugar
1 tablespoon orange flavored liqueur
6 ounces semi-sweet chocolate
2 ounces cold water
1 package unflavored gelatin
Zest (finely grated outer portion of orange rind) of 1 orange
Juice of 1 orange
1 cup cream, whipped

1   Beat eggs, egg yolks and sugar until thick and lemon colored. Add orange flavored liqueur.

2   Soften gelatin in water, add orange zest and juice and microcook on High Power 1 minute or until liquid is clear and heated through.

ORANGE CHOCOLATE MOUSSE   *continued*

3   Place chocolate in a microsafe container and micro-cook on High Power, 1 minute, stir. Continue to cook in 1 minute intervals, stirring after each cooking period, until chocolate is completely melted and smooth.

4   Combine egg mixture, melted chocolate and juice-gelatin mixture.

5   Fold in the whipped cream and gently dish into a 1 1/2 quart soufflé dish.

6   Chill at least 4 hours. Serve in stemmed goblets with a dollop of whipped cream and/or chocolate leaves (see index).

Serves 4-6

*At a family gathering my mother really impressed us with
this flaming dessert. Now the microwave makes it so much
easier to prepare. Wouldn't she be amazed?*

PEARS WITH FLAMING RASPBERRY SAUCE

2 29-ounce cans pear halves (12 pear halves)
1 3-ounce package cream cheese
1 tablespoon sugar
1/4 cup chopped walnuts
Fresh mint leaves for garnish

<u>Raspberry Sauce</u>:

1/4 cup water
1 tablespoon cornstarch
1 tablespoon sugar
1 10-ounce package frozen raspberries, undrained
1/4 cup brandy

1 Unwrap cream cheese bar and place in a microsafe
bowl. Microcook on High Power 1 minute to soften.
Combine the cream cheese, sugar and walnuts with
a little of the pear syrup. Mix to spreading consistency.

2 Drain pear halves and blot with paper towels. Spread
a thin layer of cream cheese mixture on flat side of
pear half. Top with another pear half, press together
and refrigerate.

PEARS WITH FLAMING RASPBERRY SAUCE

continued

3   For the Flaming Raspberry Sauce, combine water,
sugar and cornstarch in a microsafe bowl. Partially
thaw the frozen raspberries by placing in a microsafe
bowl and microcooking on High Power 3-4 minutes.

4   Combine undrained thawed raspberries with the
cornstarch mixture. Microcook on High Power 2
minutes. Stir and continue to cook in 2 minute intervals until thickened and lump free. Stir well after
each cooking period (takes 4-6 minutes). When
sauce is as thick as you wish, press through a sieve to
remove seeds.

5   When ready to serve, place pears on serving plates.
Microwave sauce on High 2-3 minutes until warm.
Pour brandy into a microsafe bowl and microcook on
High Power for 45 seconds, just to warm it. Pour
brandy over the sauce that has been placed in a
decorative serving bowl and serve at the table,
igniting the sauce and ladling over the pears while
flaming. Garnish with fresh mint leaves. (Make
certain your candles are lit for this impressive dessert).

Serves 6

Another flaming dessert for a special dinner party.

BANANAS FOSTER

1/4 cup butter or margarine
6 bananas
1/4 cup brown sugar, packed
1/4 teaspoon cinnamon
1/2 cup rum
1/2 gallon rich vanilla ice cream
Chopped nuts for garnish

1   Place butter in a microsafe and flameproof casserole or oval au gratin dish that may also be used as the serving dish. Microcook on High Power 30 seconds.

2   Peel and slice bananas lengthwise and cut into 1 inch chunks.

3   Add brown sugar and cinnamon to melted butter and stir to blend. Add bananas and stir gently to coat. Microcook on High Power 3-4 minutes or until sugar is dissolved. Let stand.

4   Pour rum into a microsafe bowl and microcook for 30 seconds to warm. Pour over bananas and take to table. Before serving ignite the dish. When flame subsides, sprinkle with chopped nuts.

5   To serve, scoop ice cream into large goblets and spoon the hot banana sauce over.

Serves: 10-12

Ice cream in the microwave? You'll love the rich flavor of this custard based frozen delight.

BUTTER PECAN ICE CREAM

1/2 cup pecans, coarsely broken
2 tablespoons butter or margarine
3/4 cup milk
3/4 cup whipping cream
3 egg yolks
1/3 cup sugar
1 teaspoon flour
1 teaspoon vanilla extract

1   Place pecan pieces and butter in a microsafe bowl. Microcook on High Power 2-3 minutes or until the nuts are nicely toasted. Reserve.

2   Place the milk and cream in a microsafe bowl and microcook for 3-4 minutes or until simmering.

3   Combine egg yolks and sugar in a microsafe bowl and add flour, mixing well. Pour hot milk and cream into egg mixture, stirring well. Microcook on High Power in 1 minute intervals, stirring after each minute of cooking. Cook until the mixture thickens into a light custard, 4-6 minutes.

4   Stir in vanilla extract and toasted pecan pieces. Cool the mixture to room temperature and freeze. (This recipe is marvelous frozen in one of the ice-and-salt-free fast-freezing ice cream makers.).

Makes 1 pint

Another microwave-easy dessert adapted from a recipe my mother used to make.

FROZEN STRAWBERRY DESSERT

1 cup flour
1/2 cup butter or margarine
1/4 cup brown sugar
1/2 cup coarsely chopped walnuts
2 egg whites
1 cup sugar
1 tablespoon lemon juice
1 teaspoon vanilla
1 10-ounce package frozen strawberries
1 cup whipping cream, whipped

1   Place flour, butter, brown sugar and nuts in a 11 x 15 microsafe baking dish. Microcook on High Power for 2 minutes. Stir well and continue to cook on High Power in 1 minute intervals, stirring after each cooking period. Cook until light brown and crumbly.

2   Combine egg whites, sugar, lemon juice, vanilla and unthawed frozen strawberries in a large mixing bowl. Beat at high speed with an electric mixer for 20 MINUTES. (do not use processor)

3   Fold whipped cream into the fluffy strawberry mixture.

4   Remove 1/4 of the crumbs and reserve. Shake remaining crumbs to distribute evenly over bottom of baking dish. Mound filling over the crumbs. and sprinkle reserved crumbs on top.

5   Cover with aluminum foil and freeze.

6   To serve, cut into squares and garnish with a cluster of fresh berries and mint leaves if you wish.

Serves 10-12

The editors of Bon Appétit magazine thought this recipe I adapted to the microwave was a good one. They printed it in the March, 1986 issue of the magazine and in their cookbook TOO BUSY TO COOK, Volume II. Turn on your microwave and try it. The presentation belies the ease of preparation.

POTS DE CRÈME

1 6-ounce package semi-sweet chocolate chips
1 egg
2 tablespoons sugar
1 teaspoon vanilla
Pinch of salt
3/4 cup milk (or 1/2 cup milk plus 1/4 cup brandy)
Whipped cream
Chocolate leaves, optional (see index for recipe)

1   Place chocolate chips, egg, sugar, vanilla and salt in the work bowl of a processor fitted with steel blade.

2   Pour milk into a microsafe bowl and microcook on High Power until just boiling, about 2 minutes.

3   With processor running, pour milk through feed tube and process until smooth, stopping occasionally to scrape down sides of work bowl.

4   Pour into pot de crème cups, 1/2 cup ramekins, or demitasse cups. Just before serving, top each with a dollop of whipped cream and a chocolate leaf.

Serves 4

13

MENU SUGGESTIONS

SOUTH OF THE BORDER DINNER
Super Simple Nachos (appetizer)
Chilli Con Queso Soup
Mexican Lasagne
Warm buttered flour tortillas
Your favorite green salad, sprinkled with broken
    corn chips
Bananas Foster

JUST VEGGIES
Artichoke Dip with butter crackers
Spaghetti Squash with Marinara Sauce
Tomato Mozzerella Melts
Vegetable Medley
Carrot Cake

'STUFFED' POTATO DINNER FOR FAMILY OR GUESTS
Microbaked Potatoes with choice of:
Taco Topping
"Souper" Fast Beef Stroganoff
Lo-Cal Cottage Cheese Topping
Dilled Oil and Vinegar Topping
Your favorite fruit or green salad
Frozen Strawberry Dessert

BRUNCH
Eggs or Asparagus Benedict with Hollandaise
Fruit skewers
English muffins
Marvelous Microwave Marmalade
Walnut Bark

SALAD SAMPLER LUNCHEON FOR A CROWD
Oriental Chicken Salad
Molded Spring Salad
Tabbouleh
Hot rolls
White Chocolate Crisps
Peanut Butter Bars

PASTA PARTY
Beef Roll-ups (appetizer)
Walnut sauced pasta
Your favorite green salad tossed with croutons
French bread
Mud Pie

FRIDAY NIGHT DINNER FOR THE FAMILY
Herbed Beef with Polenta
Wilted Greens Salad
Peanut Butter Cookies with fruit

COCKTAIL PARTY FARE
Warm Brie with Pine Nuts
Teriyaki Shish Kabob Appetizer
Brandied Chicken Liver Paté
Bacon and Walnut Appetizer Pie
Hot Crab Dip
Mexican Fondue

HOLIDAY TURKEY DINNER
Shrimp Mousse (appetizer)
Cranberry Chutney with cream cheese and crackers
   (appetizer)
Microcooked turkey with dressing
Cranberry Relish
Potatoes Romanoff
Cheese Frosted Cauliflower
Glazed Broccoli with Almonds
Your family's favorite salad
Hot rolls
Your family's favorite holiday dessert

SOUP AND SALAD FOR A WARM SUMMER DAY
Chilled Cucumber Soup with Walnuts
Calamari Salad
Hot rolls
Orange Chocolate Mousse with Chocolate Leaves

HAM DINNER
Microcooked ham
Molded Mustard Cream
Dilled Zucchini and Mushrooms
Colorful Carrots
Banana Pecan Rum Cake

LO-CAL
Terriyaki Skewers
Pine Nut Vegetable Pilaf
Eggplant Parmesan Diet Snack
Fresh fruit

DINNER WITH A FRENCH FLAIR
Shrimp Mousse (appetizer)
Warm Brie with Pine Nuts
Vichyssoise
Chicken Kiev
Jullienne of fresh vegetables microcooked with
    minced garlic and butter
Potatoes Anna
Pots de Crème with Chocolate Leaves

CHINESE
Chinese Chicken in Parchment
Scallops with Snow Peas
Super Simple Perfect Rice
Fresh fruit

EASY CHICKEN CURRY DINNER
Bacon and Pineapple Spears (Appetizer)
Chunky Chicken Curry
Super Simple Perfect Rice
Bengal Chutney
Salad greens tossed with your favorite dressing,
    mandarin oranges and toasted sesame seeds
Lemon Wedges

DINNER PARTY FARE

Prosciutto Wrapped Asparagus with Dill Mayonnaise
(appetizer)
Roasted Garlic (appetizer)
Greek Lemon Soup
Port Tenderloin with Madeira Sauce
Polenta with Cheese and Mushrooms
Vegetable Medley
Individual Fruit Tarts in Nut Crumb Crusts

AN INFORMAL, DO-AHEAD SUMMER DINNER

Chicken Bolognese Style
Marvelous Mushroom Soup
Cold Poached Salmon
Dilled Cucumber Sauce
Raisin Pecan and Wild Rice Salad
Frozen Lemon Pie

COMPANY FARE

Brandied Chicken Liver Paté (appetizer)
Proscuitto Wrapped Asparagus with Dill Mayonnaise
Wilted Greens Salad
Stuffed Chicken Breasts
Fast and Fabulous Rice Casserole
Dilled Zucchini with Almonds
Pears with Flaming Raspberry Sauce

SOUP AND SALAD

Carrot Tarragon Soup
Salad greens tossed with your favorite dressing,
croutons and Rosemary Walnuts
Hot rolls
Wedges of steamed pudding with Rum Sauce

9 DOZEN COOKIES IN A HURRY

*Your darling child forgot to tell you to have 9 dozen cookies
ready for the scout gathering at 4 this afternoon—Here is a
fast and simple solution to that request!*
White Chocolate Crisps
Crunchy Chocolate Cookies
Butterscotch Crispies

TAILGATE SALAD PICNIC
Tomato Sip
White Bean and Ham Salad
Potato Salad Niçoise
Raisin Pecan and Wild Rice Salad
French Bread
Peanut Butter Bars

DINNER SALAD MENU FOR A WARM SUMMER EVENING
Beef Salad Ole'
Individual servings of Mexican Fondue with tortilla
    chips
Fresh fruit

HOLIDAY CANDY AND DESSERT TABLE
White Chocolate Crisps
Butterscotch Crispies
Chocolate Shortbread Cookies
Lemon Wedges
Creme de Menthe Bars
Walnut Bark
Perfect Peanut Brittle
Peanut Butter Bars
Easy Almond Roca

DINNER FOR ONE
5 minute Chicken Dijon
Chopped vegetable assortment from Deli Salad Bar,
    microcooked with butter and minced garlic

A SIMPLE DINNER THAT CHILDREN OR ADULTS WILL ENJOY
Super Simple Nachos (appetizer)
Chicken Wings Ole' (appetizer)
Beef and Noodles
Corn on the Cob
Fresh Fruit cup or a green salad
Mud Pie

INDEX

INDEX

Mail Order Information

THE EVERYDAY GOURMET

Price per book (USA) $13.95
Shipping and handling per book 2.00
California Residents add sales tax per book 91

Canadian orders submit US Funds.

Autographed copy, gift wrapped with personalized
enclosure card $2.00 per book.

Make checks or money orders payable to:
CREATIVE COOKERY

Mail to: Creative Cookery
P.O. Box 437
Alamo, CA 94507

No credit cards, please.

ORDER BY MAIL

Number of copies: _____

Amount enclosed: $_____

$13.95/book + $2.00 post + CA tax $.91

(Autographed, gift wrapped $2 additional)

Mail Cookbook to:

Name _____

Address _____

City/State/Zip _____

Gift Card: TO _____

FROM _____

(cut here for first order)

✂ —

Number of copies: _____

Amount enclosed: $ _____

$13.95/book + $2.00 post + CA tax $.91

(Autographed, gift wrapped $2 additional)

Mail Cookbook to:

Name _____

Address _____

City/State/Zip _____

Gift Card: TO _____

FROM _____

ORDER BY MAIL

Number of copies: _____

Amount enclosed: $_____

$13.95/book + $2.00 post + CA tax $.91

(Autographed, gift wrapped $2 additional)

Mail Cookbook to:

Name _____

Address _____

City/State/Zip_____

Gift Card: TO _____

               FROM _____

(cut here for first order)

✂ —

Number of copies: _____

Amount enclosed: $ _____

$13.95/book + $2.00 post + CA tax $.91

(Autographed, gift wrapped $2 additional)

Mail Cookbook to:

Name _____

Address _____

City/State/Zip_____

Gift Card: TO_____

               FROM _____